EYEWITNESS VISUAL DICTIONARIES

THE VISUAL DICTIONARY *of the*

HUMAN BODY

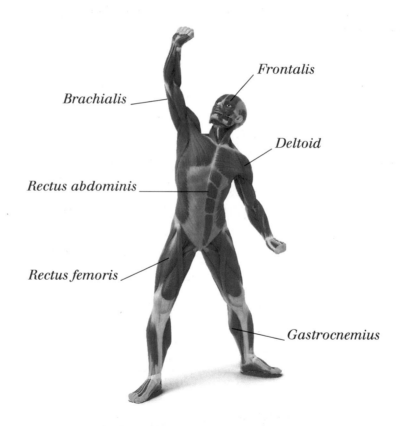

Frontalis

Brachialis

Deltoid

Rectus abdominis

Rectus femoris

Gastrocnemius

SUPERFICIAL SKELETAL MUSCLES

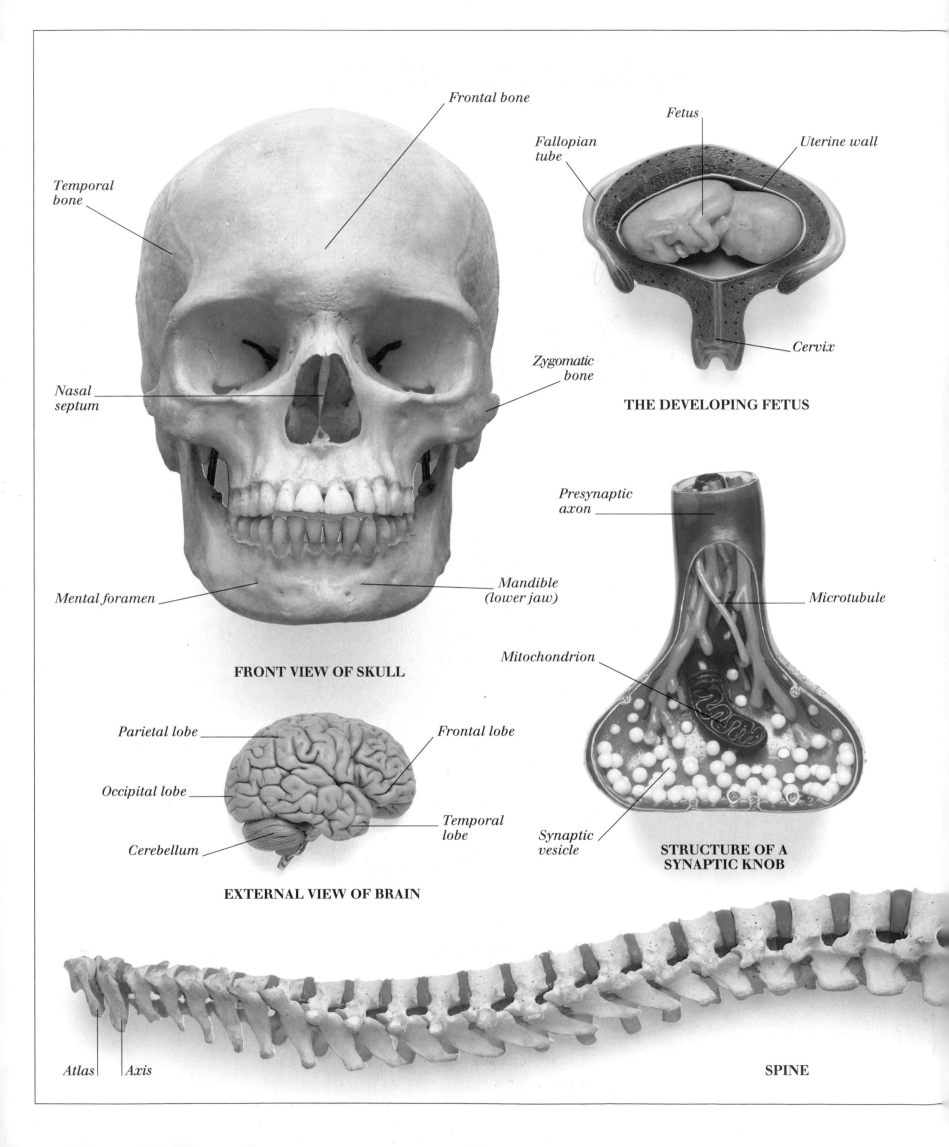

Frontal bone

Temporal bone

Nasal septum

Mental foramen

Zygomatic bone

Mandible (lower jaw)

FRONT VIEW OF SKULL

Fetus

Fallopian tube

Uterine wall

Cervix

THE DEVELOPING FETUS

Presynaptic axon

Microtubule

Mitochondrion

Synaptic vesicle

STRUCTURE OF A SYNAPTIC KNOB

Parietal lobe

Frontal lobe

Occipital lobe

Temporal lobe

Cerebellum

EXTERNAL VIEW OF BRAIN

Atlas

Axis

SPINE

EYEWITNESS VISUAL DICTIONARIES

THE VISUAL
DICTIONARY *of the*
HUMAN
BODY

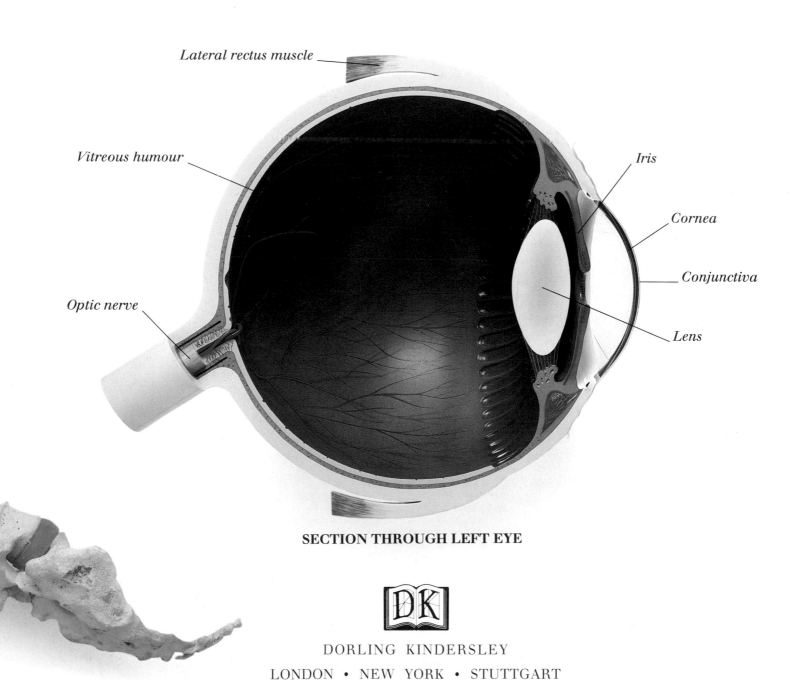

Lateral rectus muscle

Vitreous humour

Iris

Cornea

Conjunctiva

Optic nerve

Lens

SECTION THROUGH LEFT EYE

DK

DORLING KINDERSLEY

LONDON • NEW YORK • STUTTGART

A DORLING KINDERSLEY BOOK

PROJECT ART EDITOR BRYN WALLS
DESIGNERS DUNCAN BROWN, SIMONE END, NICKI LIDDIARD

PROJECT EDITOR MARY LINDSAY
CONSULTANT EDITORS RICHARD CUMMINS, FRCS, DR FIONA PAYNE, DR FRANCES WILLIAMS

SERIES ART EDITOR PAUL WILKINSON
ART DIRECTOR CHEZ PICTHALL
MANAGING EDITOR RUTH MIDGLEY

PHOTOGRAPHY PETER CHADWICK, GEOFF DANN, DAVE KING

PRODUCTION HILARY STEPHENS

ANATOMICAL MODELS SUPPLIED BY SOMSO MODELLE, COBURG, GERMANY

Superior vena cava   Aorta

Right ventricle   Left ventricle

CIRCULATORY SYSTEM OF HEART AND LUNGS

FIRST PUBLISHED IN GREAT BRITAIN IN 1991
BY DORLING KINDERSLEY LIMITED,
9 HENRIETTA STREET, LONDON WC2E 8PS

REPRINTED 1992
REPRINTED 1993
REPRINTED 1995

A CIP CATALOGUE RECORD FOR THIS BOOK IS AVAILABLE FROM THE BRITISH LIBRARY

ISBN 0-86318-700-5

REPRODUCED BY GRB GRAFICA, VERONA, ITALY
PRINTED AND BOUND BY ARNOLDO MONDADORI, VERONA, ITALY

Contents

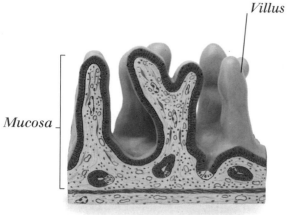

Villus

Mucosa

INTERNAL SURFACE OF JEJUNUM

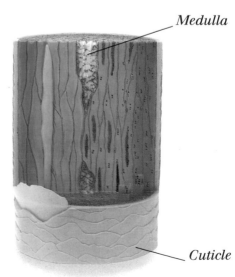

Metatarsal

Calcaneus

BONES OF FOOT

Middle phalanx

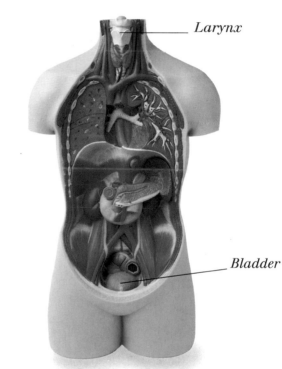

Larynx

Bladder

**CHEST AND ABDOMINAL CAVITIES
WITH SOME ORGANS REMOVED**

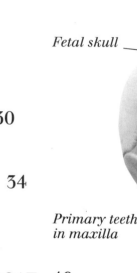

Fetal skull

*Primary teeth
in maxilla*

**DEVELOPMENT OF
TEETH IN A FETUS**

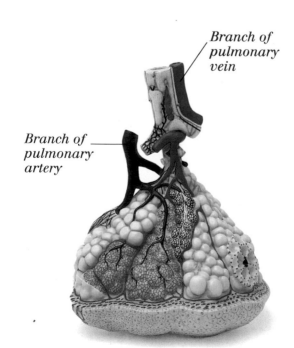

*Branch of
pulmonary
vein*

*Branch of
pulmonary
artery*

BRONCHIOLE WITH LOBULE

Medulla

Cuticle

SECTION OF HAIR

The human body

ALTHOUGH THERE IS enormous variation between the external appearances of humans, all bodies contain the same basic features. The outward form of the human body depends on the size of the skeleton, the shape of the muscles, the thickness of the fat layer beneath the skin, the elasticity or sagginess of the skin, and the person's age and sex. Males tend to be taller than females, with broader shoulders, more body hair, and a different pattern of fat deposits under the skin; the female body tends to be less muscular and has a shallower and wider pelvis to allow for childbirth.

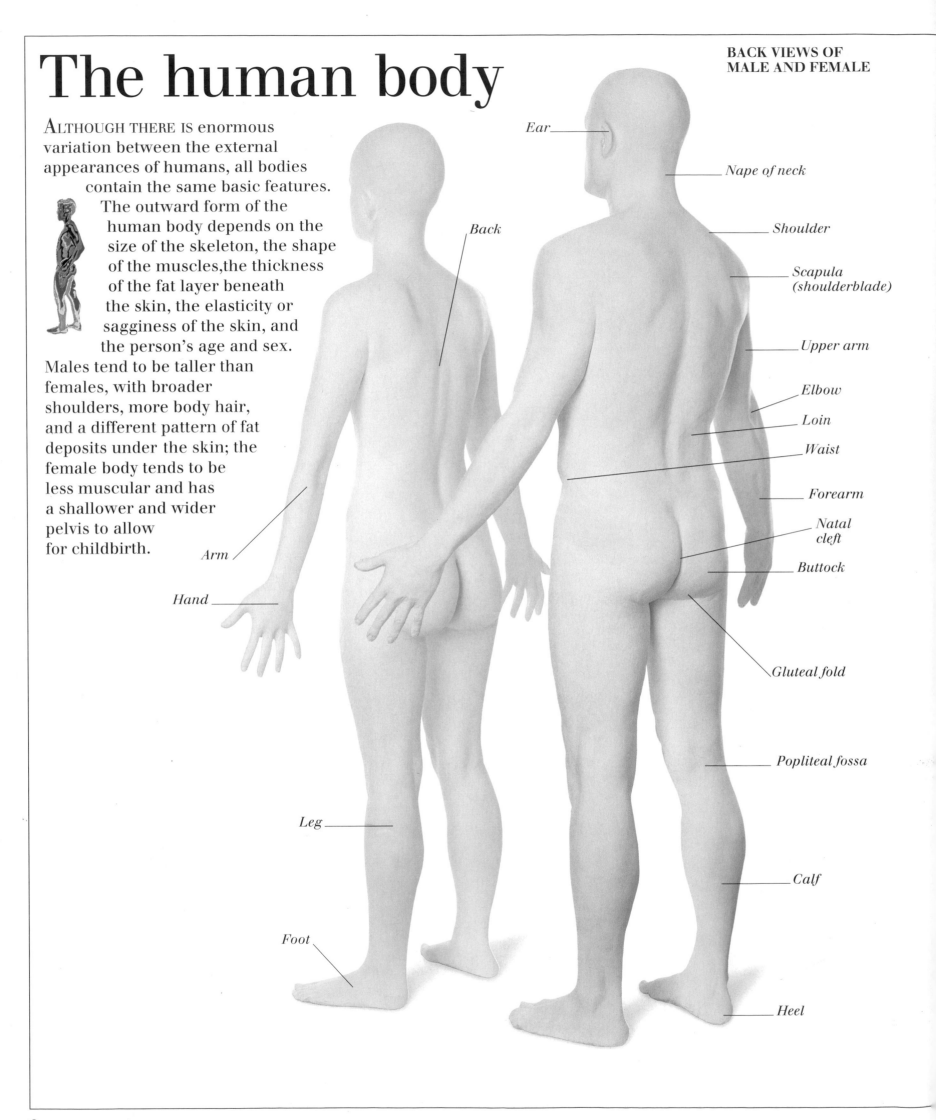

Ear

Nape of neck

Shoulder

Scapula (shoulderblade)

Back

Upper arm

Elbow

Loin

Waist

Forearm

Natal cleft

Buttock

Arm

Gluteal fold

Hand

Popliteal fossa

Leg

Calf

Foot

Heel

**FRONT VIEWS OF
MALE AND FEMALE**

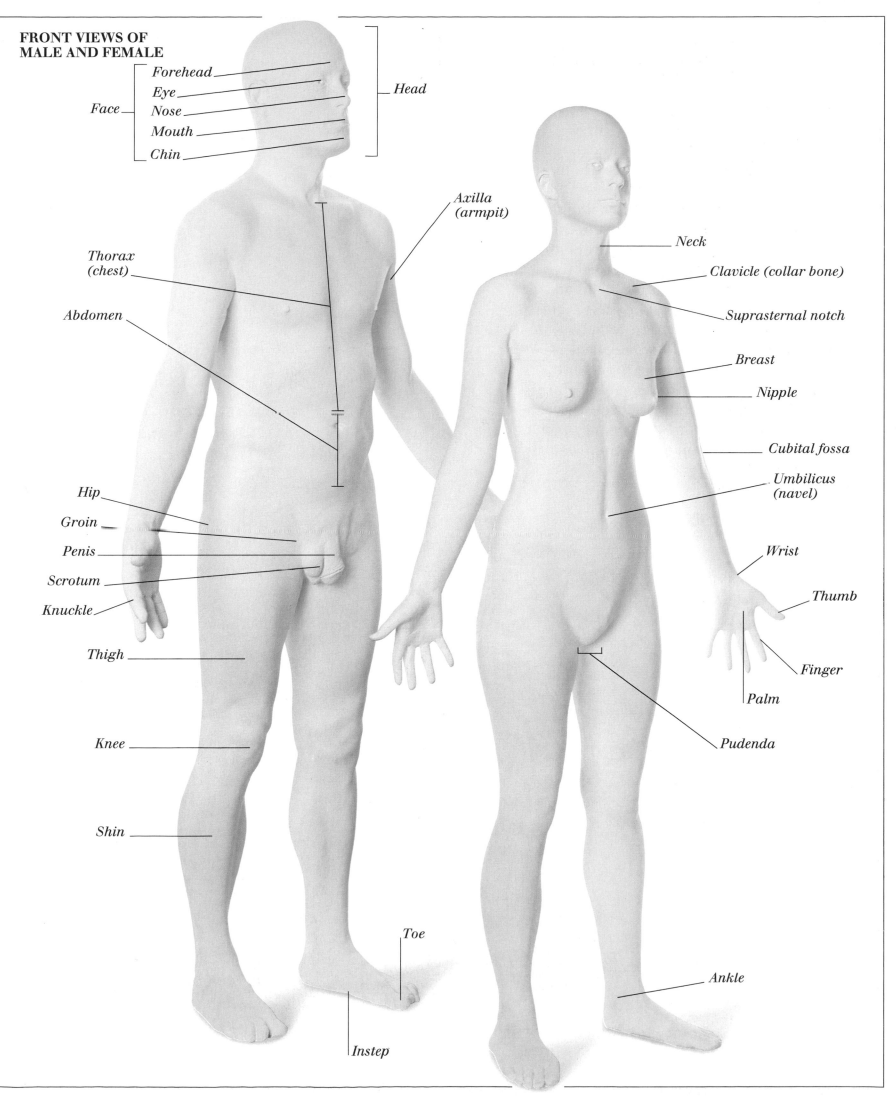

Forehead

Eye

Face

Nose

Mouth

Chin

Head

Axilla
(armpit)

Neck

Clavicle (collar bone)

Suprasternal notch

Thorax
(chest)

Abdomen

Breast

Nipple

Cubital fossa

Umbilicus
(navel)

Hip

Groin

Penis

Scrotum

Knuckle

Wrist

Thumb

Finger

Thigh

Palm

Knee

Pudenda

Shin

Toe

Ankle

Instep

Head

IN A NEWBORN BABY, the head accounts for one-quarter of the total body length; by adulthood, the proportion has reduced to one-eighth. Contained in the head are the body's main sense organs: eyes, ears, olfactory nerves that detect smells, and the taste buds of the tongue. Signals from these organs pass to the body's great coordination centre: the brain, housed in the protective, bony dome of the skull. Hair on the head insulates against heat loss, and adult males also grow thick facial hair. The face has three important openings: two nostrils through which air passes, and the mouth, which takes in nourishment and helps form speech. Although all heads are basically similar, differences in the size, shape, and colour of features produce an infinite variety of appearances.

SIDE VIEW OF EXTERNAL FEATURES OF HEAD

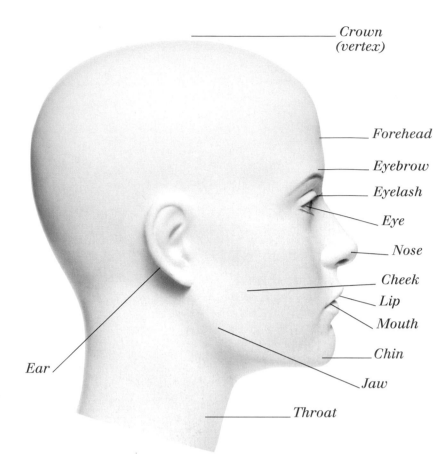

Crown (vertex)

Forehead

Eyebrow

Eyelash

Eye

Nose

Cheek

Lip

Mouth

Chin

Jaw

Throat

Ear

SECTION THROUGH HEAD

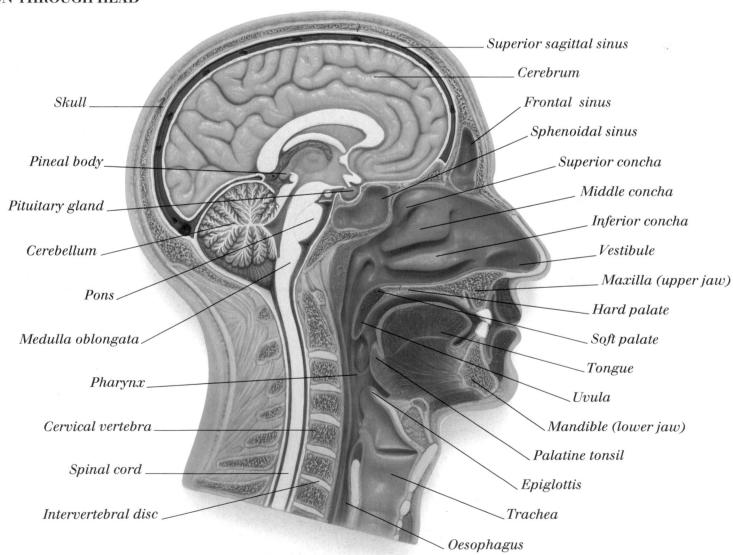

Superior sagittal sinus

Cerebrum

Frontal sinus

Sphenoidal sinus

Superior concha

Middle concha

Inferior concha

Vestibule

Maxilla (upper jaw)

Hard palate

Soft palate

Tongue

Uvula

Mandible (lower jaw)

Palatine tonsil

Epiglottis

Trachea

Oesophagus

Skull

Pineal body

Pituitary gland

Cerebellum

Pons

Medulla oblongata

Pharynx

Cervical vertebra

Spinal cord

Intervertebral disc

**FRONT VIEW OF EXTERNAL
FEATURES OF HEAD**

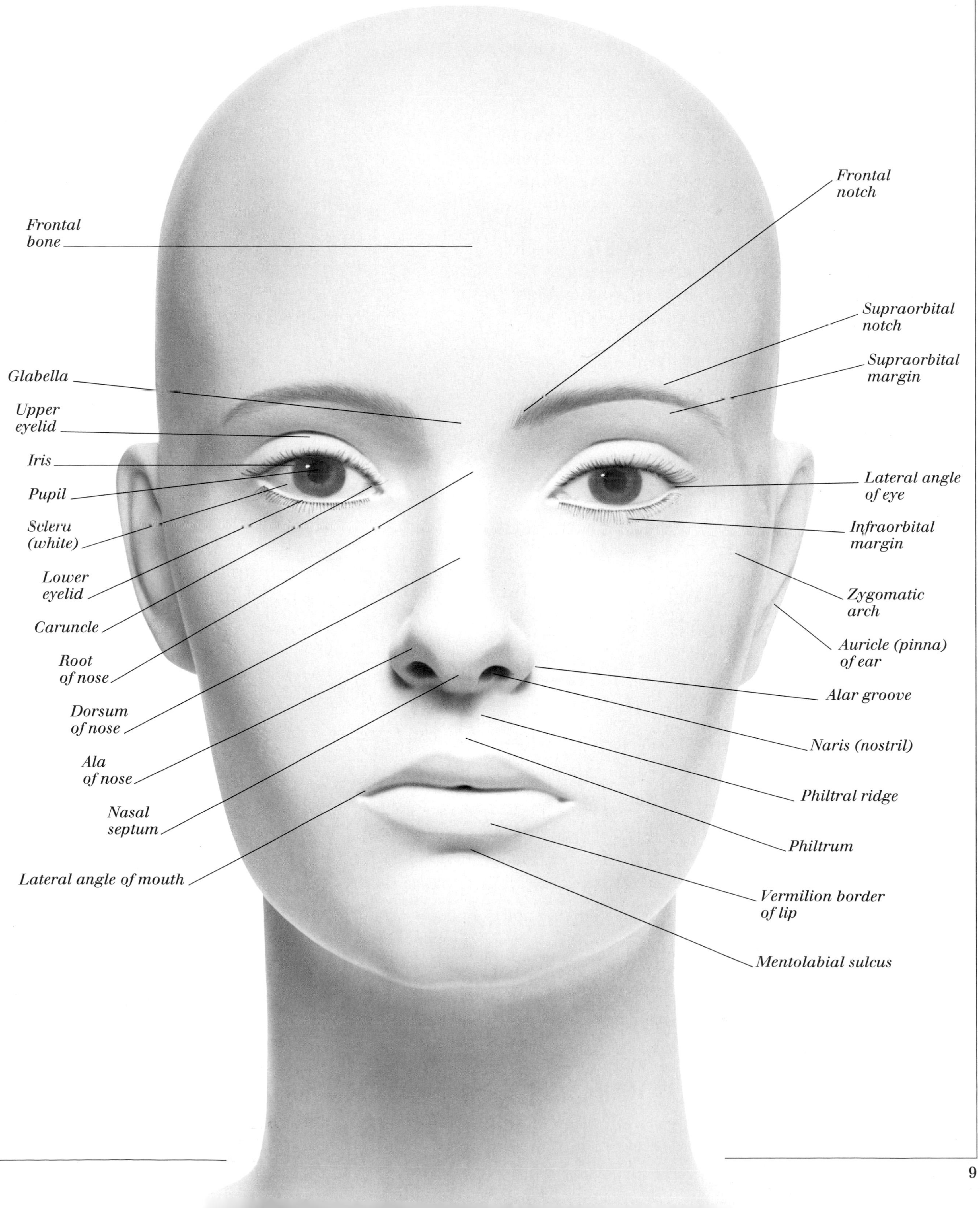

Frontal
notch

Supraorbital
notch

Supraorbital
margin

Frontal
bone

Glabella

Upper
eyelid

Iris

Pupil

Sclera
(white)

Lower
eyelid

Caruncle

Root
of nose

Dorsum
of nose

Ala
of nose

Nasal
septum

Lateral angle of mouth

Lateral angle
of eye

Infraorbital
margin

Zygomatic
arch

Auricle (pinna)
of ear

Alar groove

Naris (nostril)

Philtral ridge

Philtrum

Vermilion border
of lip

Mentolabial sulcus

Body organs

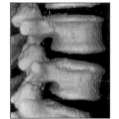

ALL THE VITAL BODY ORGANS except for the brain are enclosed within the trunk or torso (the body apart from the head and limbs). The trunk contains two large cavities separated by a muscular sheet called the diaphragm. The upper cavity, known as the thorax or chest cavity, contains the heart and lungs. The lower cavity, called the abdominal cavity, contains the stomach, intestines, liver, and pancreas, which all play a role in digesting food. Also within the trunk are the kidneys and bladder, which are part of the urinary system, and the reproductive organs, which hold the seeds of new human life. Modern imaging techniques, such as contrast X-rays and different types of scans, make it possible to see and study body organs without the need to cut through their protective coverings of skin, fat, muscle, and bone.

MAJOR INTERNAL STRUCTURES

Thyroid gland

Larynx

Heart

Right lung

Left lung

Diaphragm

Liver

Stomach

Large intestine

Small intestine

Greater omentum

IMAGING THE BODY

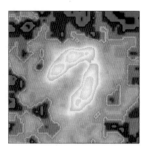

SCINTIGRAM OF HEART CHAMBERS

ANGIOGRAM OF RIGHT LUNG

CONTRAST X-RAY OF GALLBLADDER

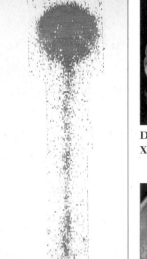

SCINTIGRAM OF NERVOUS SYSTEM

DOUBLE CONTRAST X-RAY OF COLON

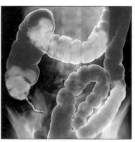

ULTRASOUND SCAN OF TWINS IN UTERUS

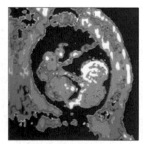

ANGIOGRAM OF KIDNEYS

ANGIOGRAM OF ARTERIES OF HEAD

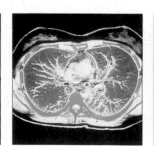

CT SCAN THROUGH FEMALE CHEST

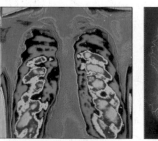

THERMOGRAM OF CHEST REGION

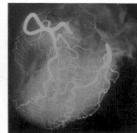

ANGIOGRAM OF ARTERIES OF HEART

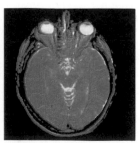

MRI SCAN THROUGH HEAD AT EYE LEVEL

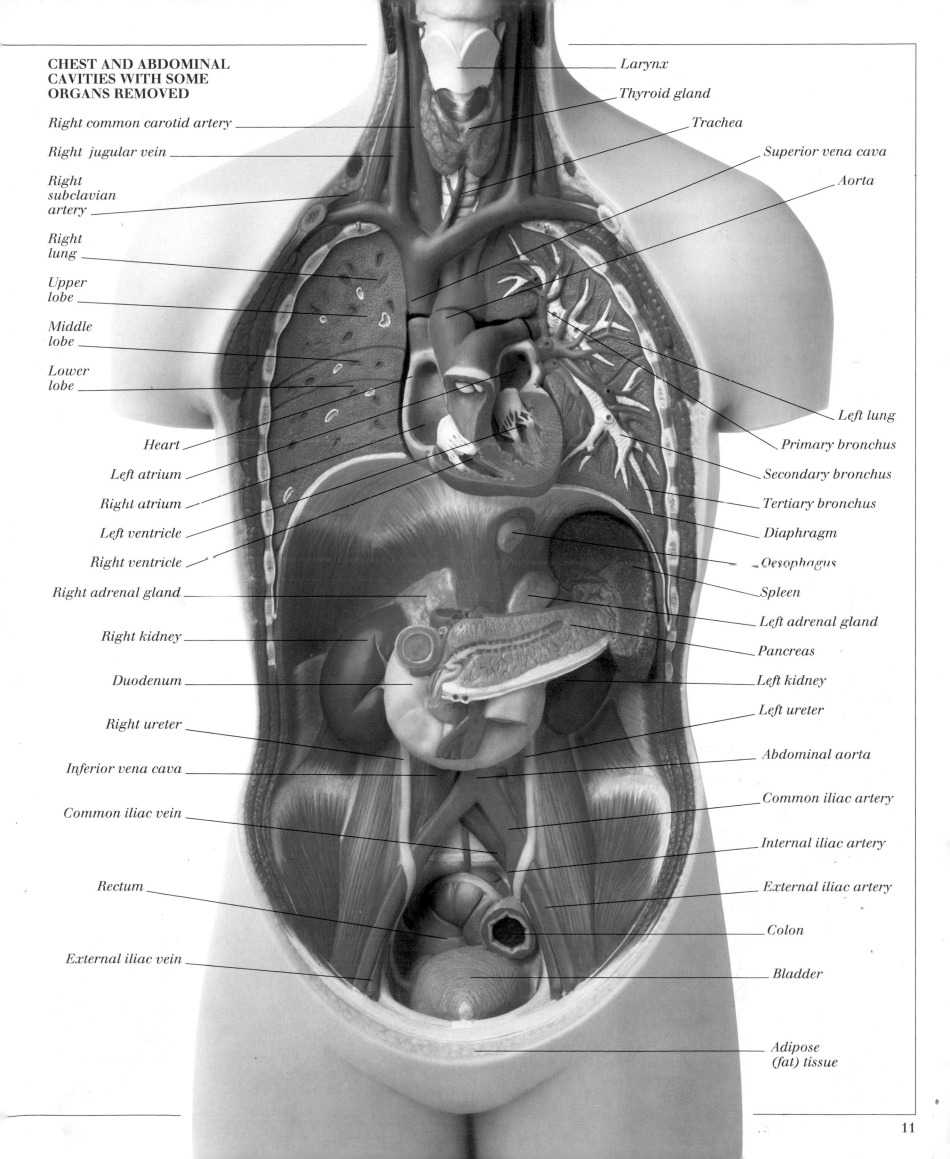

**CHEST AND ABDOMINAL
CAVITIES WITH SOME
ORGANS REMOVED**

Right common carotid artery

Right jugular vein

Right subclavian artery

Right lung

Upper lobe

Middle lobe

Lower lobe

Heart

Left atrium

Right atrium

Left ventricle

Right ventricle

Right adrenal gland

Right kidney

Duodenum

Right ureter

Inferior vena cava

Common iliac vein

Rectum

External iliac vein

Larynx

Thyroid gland

Trachea

Superior vena cava

Aorta

Left lung

Primary bronchus

Secondary bronchus

Tertiary bronchus

Diaphragm

Oesophagus

Spleen

Left adrenal gland

Pancreas

Left kidney

Left ureter

Abdominal aorta

Common iliac artery

Internal iliac artery

External iliac artery

Colon

Bladder

Adipose (fat) tissue

11

Body cells

EVERYONE IS MADE UP OF BILLIONS OF CELLS, which are the basic structural units of the body. Bones, muscles, nerves, skin, blood, and all other body tissues are formed from different types of cells. Each cell has a specific function but works with other types of cells to perform the enormous number of tasks needed to sustain life. Most body cells have a similar basic structure. Each cell has an outer layer (called the cell membrane) and contains a fluid material (cytoplasm). Within the cytoplasm are many specialized structures (organelles). The most important organelle is the nucleus, which contains vital genetic material and acts as the cell's control centre.

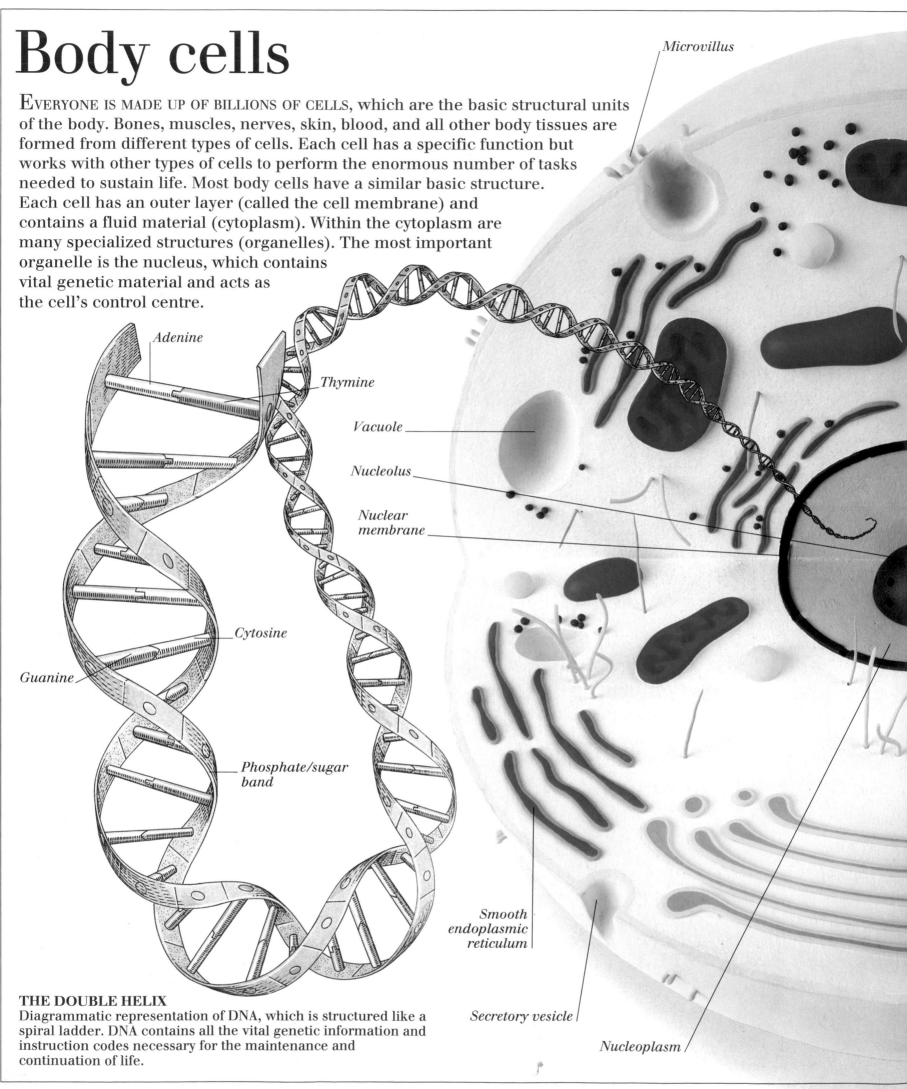

Microvillus

Adenine

Thymine

Vacuole

Nucleolus

Nuclear membrane

Cytosine

Guanine

Phosphate/sugar band

Smooth endoplasmic reticulum

THE DOUBLE HELIX
Diagrammatic representation of DNA, which is structured like a spiral ladder. DNA contains all the vital genetic information and instruction codes necessary for the maintenance and continuation of life.

Secretory vesicle

Nucleoplasm

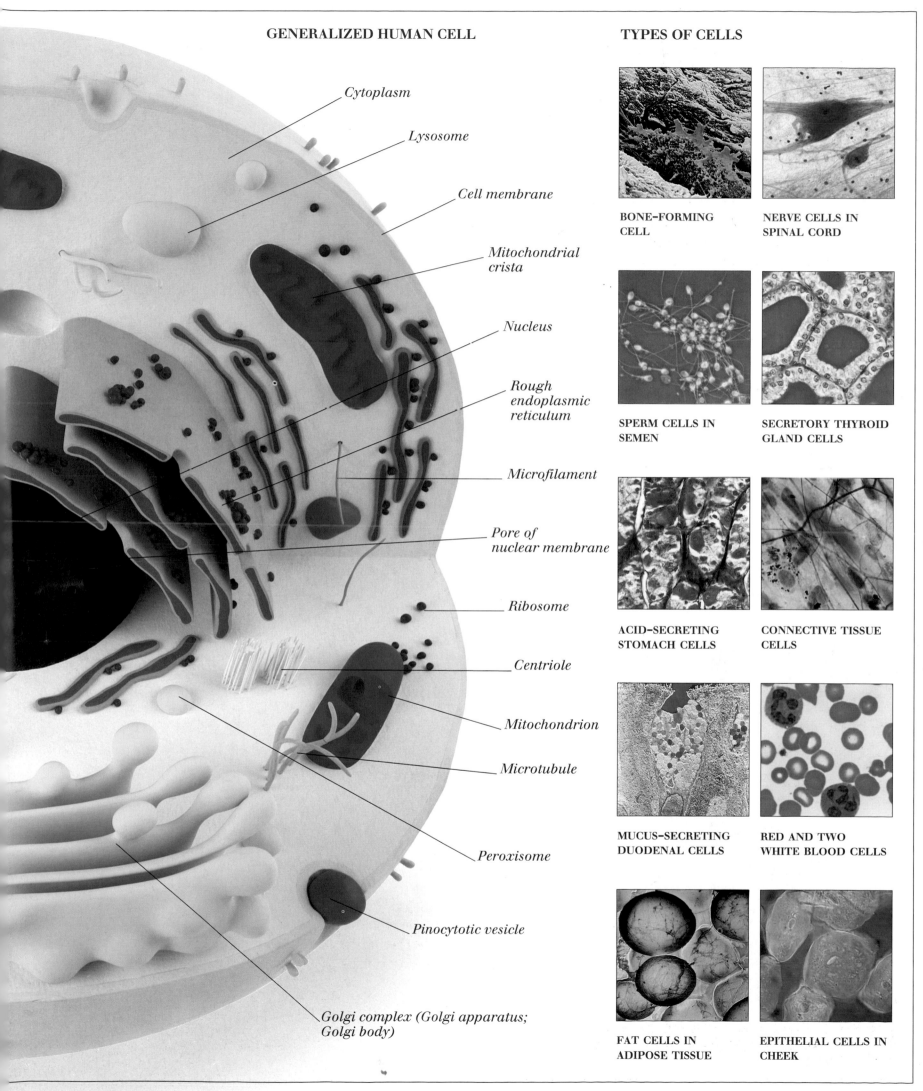

GENERALIZED HUMAN CELL

Cytoplasm

Lysosome

Cell membrane

Mitochondrial crista

Nucleus

Rough endoplasmic reticulum

Microfilament

Pore of nuclear membrane

Ribosome

Centriole

Mitochondrion

Microtubule

Peroxisome

Pinocytotic vesicle

Golgi complex (Golgi apparatus; Golgi body)

TYPES OF CELLS

BONE-FORMING CELL

NERVE CELLS IN SPINAL CORD

SPERM CELLS IN SEMEN

SECRETORY THYROID GLAND CELLS

ACID-SECRETING STOMACH CELLS

CONNECTIVE TISSUE CELLS

MUCUS-SECRETING DUODENAL CELLS

RED AND TWO WHITE BLOOD CELLS

FAT CELLS IN ADIPOSE TISSUE

EPITHELIAL CELLS IN CHEEK

Skeleton

THE SKELETON IS A MOBILE FRAMEWORK made up of 206 bones, approximately half of which are in the hands and feet. Although individual bones are rigid, the skeleton as a whole is remarkably flexible and allows the human body a huge range of movement. The skeleton serves as an anchorage for the skeletal muscles, and as a protective cage for the body's internal organs. Female bones are usually smaller and lighter than male bones, and the female pelvis is shallower and has a wider cavity.

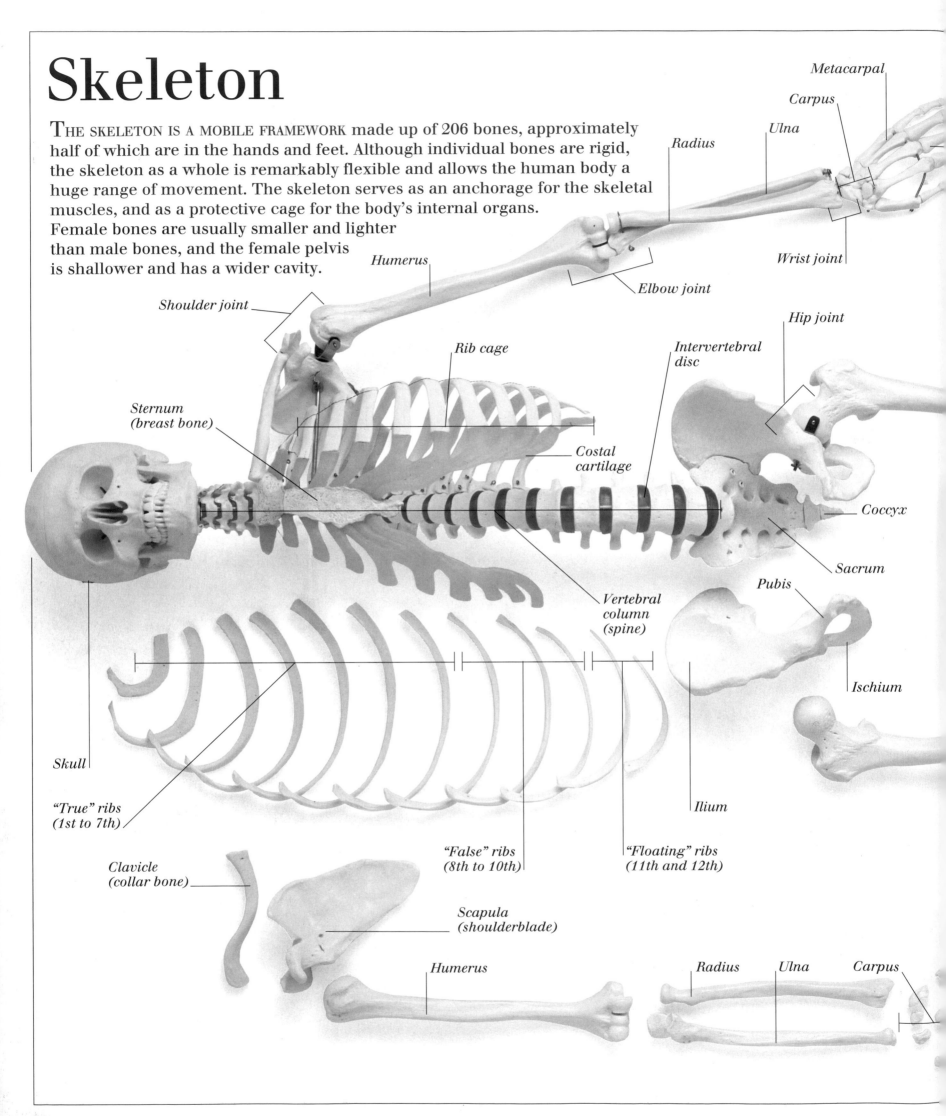

Metacarpal

Carpus

Ulna

Radius

Wrist joint

Humerus

Elbow joint

Hip joint

Shoulder joint

Rib cage

Intervertebral disc

Sternum (breast bone)

Costal cartilage

Coccyx

Sacrum

Pubis

Vertebral column (spine)

Ischium

Skull

"True" ribs (1st to 7th)

Ilium

Clavicle (collar bone)

"False" ribs (8th to 10th)

"Floating" ribs (11th and 12th)

Scapula (shoulderblade)

Humerus

Radius

Ulna

Carpus

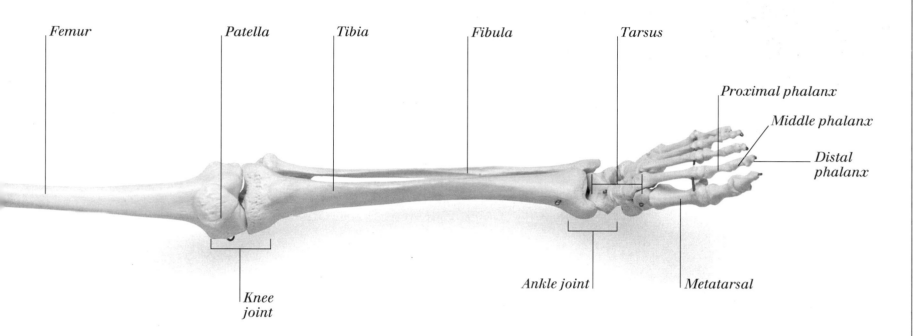

Distal phalanx

Middle phalanx

Proximal phalanx

Femur

Patella

Tibia

Fibula

Tarsus

Proximal phalanx

Middle phalanx

Distal phalanx

Ankle joint

Metatarsal

Knee joint

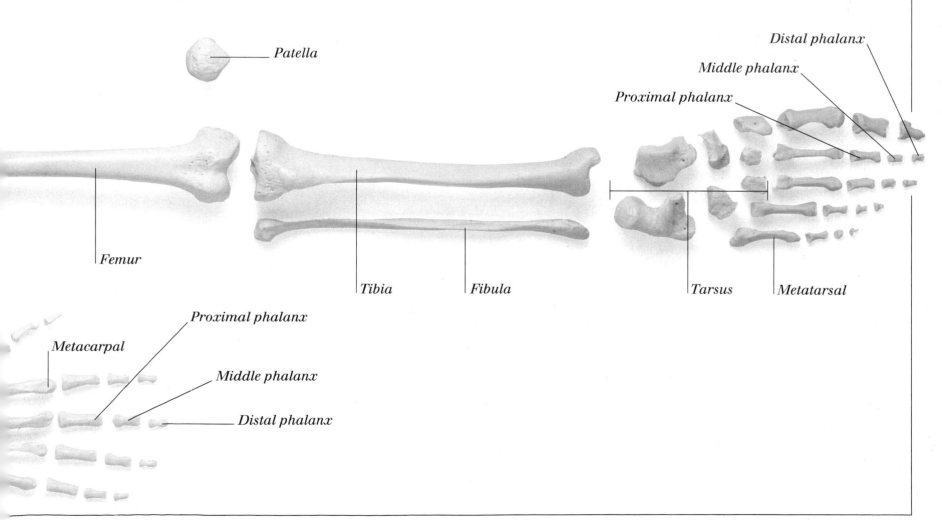

Patella

Distal phalanx

Middle phalanx

Proximal phalanx

Femur

Tibia

Fibula

Tarsus

Metatarsal

Proximal phalanx

Metacarpal

Middle phalanx

Distal phalanx

Skull

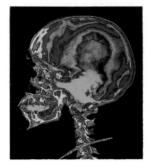

THE SKULL is the most complicated bony structure of the body but every feature serves a purpose. Internally, the main hollow chamber of the skull has three levels that support the brain, with every bump and hollow corresponding to the shape of the brain. Underneath and towards the back of the skull is a large round hole, the foramen magnum, through which the spinal cord passes. To the front of this are many smaller openings through which nerves, arteries, and veins pass to and from the brain. The roof of the skull is formed from four thin, curved bones that are firmly fixed together from the age of about two years. At the front of the skull are the two orbits, which contain the eyeballs, and a central hole for the airway of the nose. The jaw bone hinges on either side at ear level.

RIGHT SIDE VIEW OF A FETAL SKULL

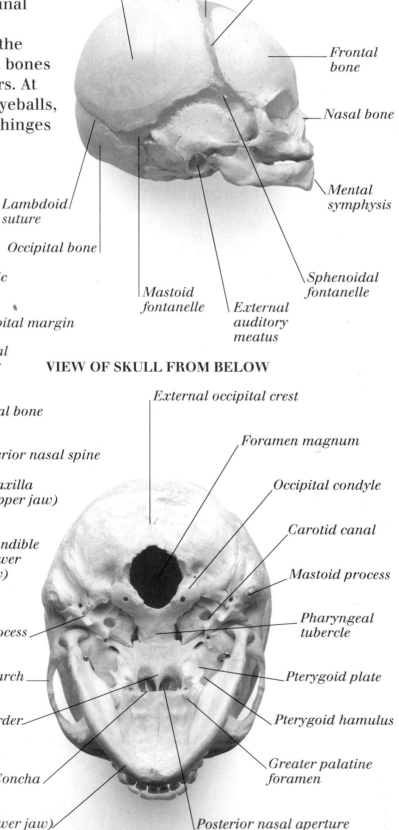

- Anterior fontanelle
- Parietal bone
- Coronal suture
- Frontal bone
- Nasal bone
- Mental symphysis
- Lambdoid suture
- Occipital bone
- Sphenoidal fontanelle
- Mastoid fontanelle
- External auditory meatus

RIGHT SIDE VIEW OF SKULL

- Coronal suture
- Frontal bone
- Greater wing of sphenoid bone
- Frontozygomatic suture
- Parietal bone
- Supraorbital margin
- Squamous suture
- Orbital cavity
- Nasal bone
- Anterior nasal spine
- Maxilla (upper jaw)
- Lambdoid suture
- Occipital bone
- Mandible (lower jaw)
- Temporal bone
- External auditory meatus
- Mastoid process
- Condyle
- Coronoid process
- Zygomatic bone
- Mental foramen

VIEW OF SKULL FROM BELOW

- External occipital crest
- Foramen magnum
- Occipital condyle
- Carotid canal
- Mastoid process
- Pharyngeal tubercle
- Pterygoid plate
- Styloid process
- Zygomatic arch
- Pterygoid hamulus
- Posterior border of vomer
- Greater palatine foramen
- Concha
- Mandible (lower jaw)
- Posterior nasal aperture

16

FRONT VIEW OF SKULL

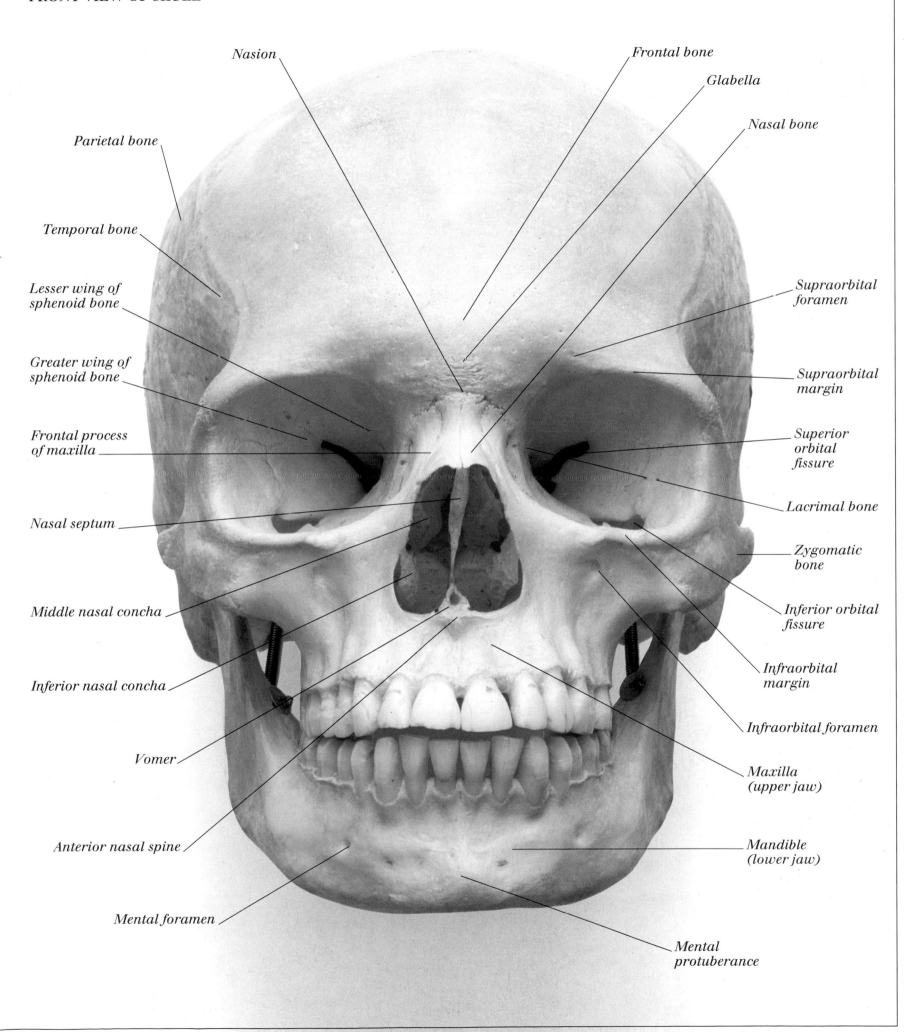

Nasion

Frontal bone

Glabella

Nasal bone

Parietal bone

Temporal bone

Lesser wing of
sphenoid bone

Supraorbital
foramen

Greater wing of
sphenoid bone

Supraorbital
margin

Frontal process
of maxilla

Superior
orbital
fissure

Nasal septum

Lacrimal bone

Middle nasal concha

Zygomatic
bone

Inferior nasal concha

Inferior orbital
fissure

Vomer

Infraorbital
margin

Anterior nasal spine

Infraorbital foramen

Maxilla
(upper jaw)

Mental foramen

Mandible
(lower jaw)

Mental
protuberance

Spine

THE SPINE (OR VERTEBRAL COLUMN) has two main functions: it serves as a protective surrounding for the delicate spinal cord and forms the supporting back bone of the skeleton. The spine consists of 24 separate differently shaped bones (vertebrae) with a curved, triangular bone (the sacrum) at the bottom. The sacrum is made up of fused vertebrae; at its lower end is a small tail-like structure made up of tiny bones collectively called the coccyx. Between each pair of vertebrae is a disc of cartilage that cushions the bones during movement. The top two vertebrae differ in appearance from the others and work as a pair: the first, called the atlas, rotates around a stout vertical peg on the second, the axis. This arrangement allows the skull to move freely up and down, and from side to side.

SPINE DIVIDED INTO VERTEBRAL SECTIONS — FRONT

Cervical vertebrae

Thoracic vertebrae

Lumbar vertebrae

Sacral vertebrae

Coccygeal vertebrae

TYPES OF VERTEBRAE (VIEWED FROM ABOVE)

ATLAS

Anterior arch
Lateral mass with superior articular facet
Posterior arch
Anterior tubercle
Posterior tubercle
Vertebral foramen
Transverse foramen
Transverse process

AXIS

Facet
Dens
Vertebral foramen
Spinous process
Lamina
Transverse process and foramen

CERVICAL VERTEBRA

Body
Superior articular process
Anterior tubercle
Spinous process
Vertebral foramen
Posterior tubercle
Transverse foramen

SKULL AND SPINE

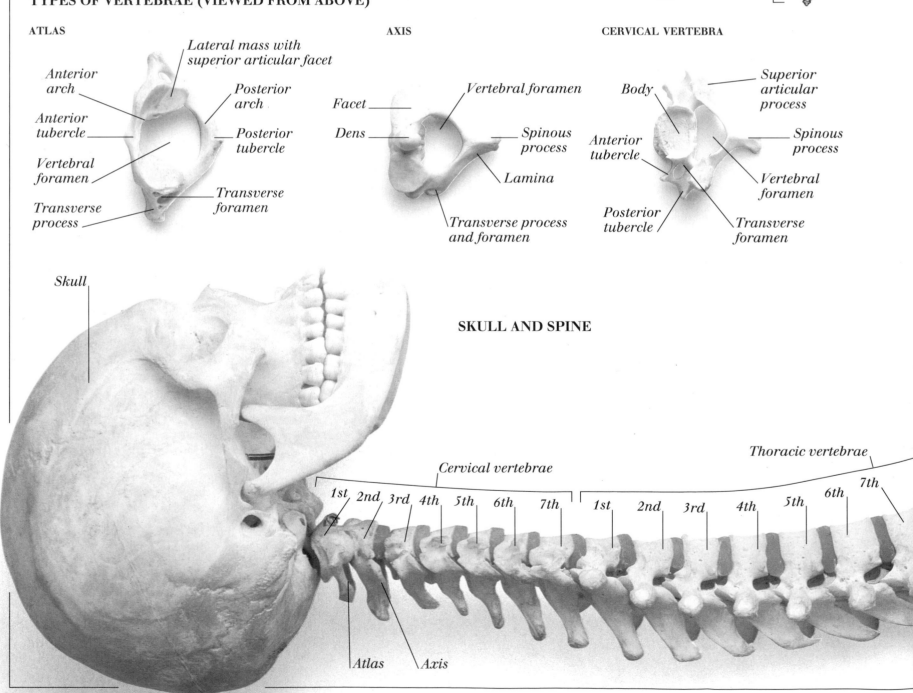

Skull

Cervical vertebrae
1st 2nd 3rd 4th 5th 6th 7th

Thoracic vertebrae
1st 2nd 3rd 4th 5th 6th 7th

Atlas Axis

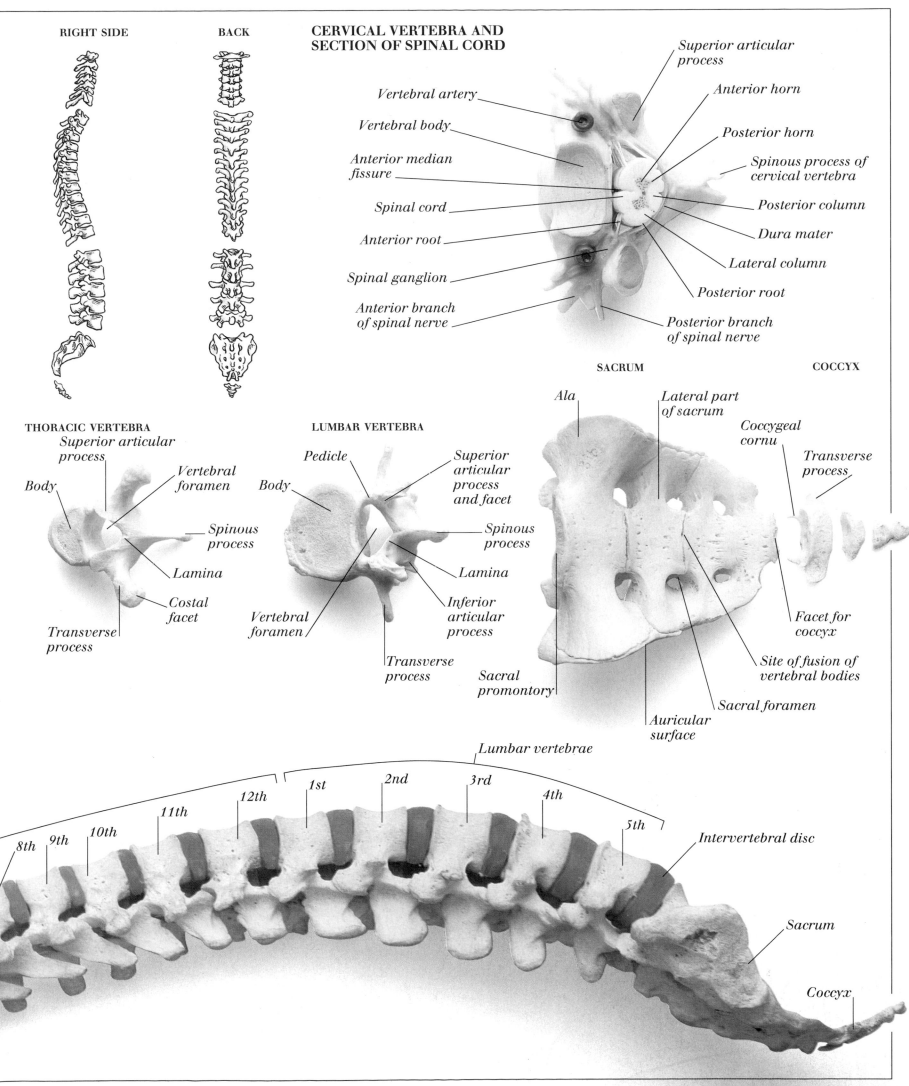

RIGHT SIDE

BACK

CERVICAL VERTEBRA AND SECTION OF SPINAL CORD

Vertebral artery

Vertebral body

Anterior median fissure

Spinal cord

Anterior root

Spinal ganglion

Anterior branch of spinal nerve

Superior articular process

Anterior horn

Posterior horn

Spinous process of cervical vertebra

Posterior column

Dura mater

Lateral column

Posterior root

Posterior branch of spinal nerve

THORACIC VERTEBRA

Superior articular process

Body

Vertebral foramen

Spinous process

Lamina

Costal facet

Transverse process

LUMBAR VERTEBRA

Pedicle

Body

Superior articular process and facet

Spinous process

Lamina

Inferior articular process

Vertebral foramen

Transverse process

SACRUM

Ala

Lateral part of sacrum

Sacral promontory

Auricular surface

Sacral foramen

Site of fusion of vertebral bodies

COCCYX

Coccygeal cornu

Transverse process

Facet for coccyx

Lumbar vertebrae

8th 9th 10th 11th 12th 1st 2nd 3rd 4th 5th

Intervertebral disc

Sacrum

Coccyx

Bones and joints

BONES FORM the body's hard, strong skeletal framework. Each bone has a hard, compact exterior surrounding a spongy, lighter interior. The long bones of the arms and legs, such as the femur (thigh bone), have a central cavity containing bone marrow. Bones are composed chiefly of calcium, phosphorus, and a fibrous substance known as collagen. Bones meet at joints, which are of several different types. For example, the hip is a ball-and-socket joint that allows the femur a wide range of movement, whereas finger joints are simple hinge joints that allow only bending and straightening. Joints are held in place by bands of tissue called ligaments. Movement of joints is facilitated by the smooth hyaline cartilage that covers the bone ends and by the synovial membrane that lines and lubricates the joint.

LIGAMENTS SURROUNDING HIP JOINT

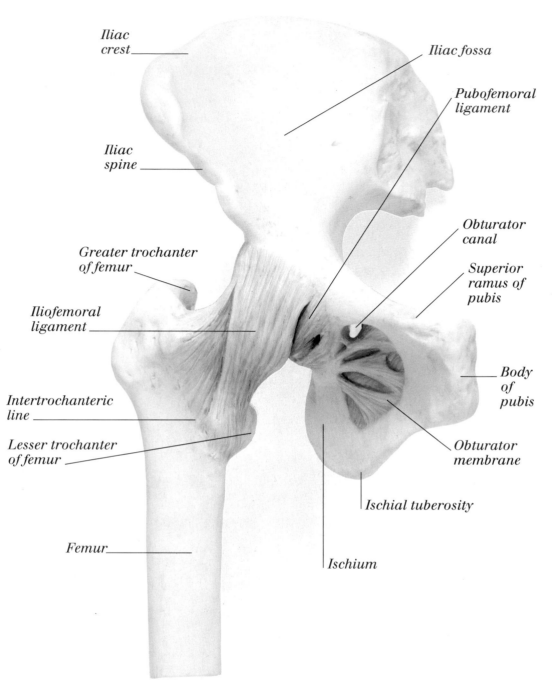

Iliac crest

Iliac spine

Greater trochanter of femur

Iliofemoral ligament

Intertrochanteric line

Lesser trochanter of femur

Femur

Iliac fossa

Pubofemoral ligament

Obturator canal

Superior ramus of pubis

Body of pubis

Obturator membrane

Ischial tuberosity

Ischium

SECTION THROUGH LEFT FEMUR

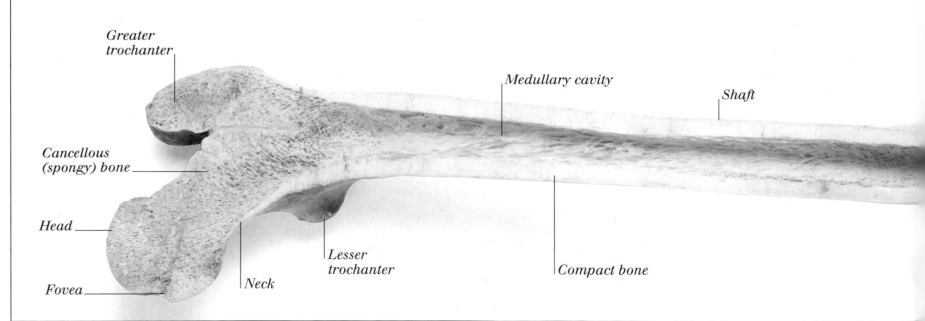

Greater trochanter

Cancellous (spongy) bone

Head

Fovea

Neck

Lesser trochanter

Medullary cavity

Compact bone

Shaft

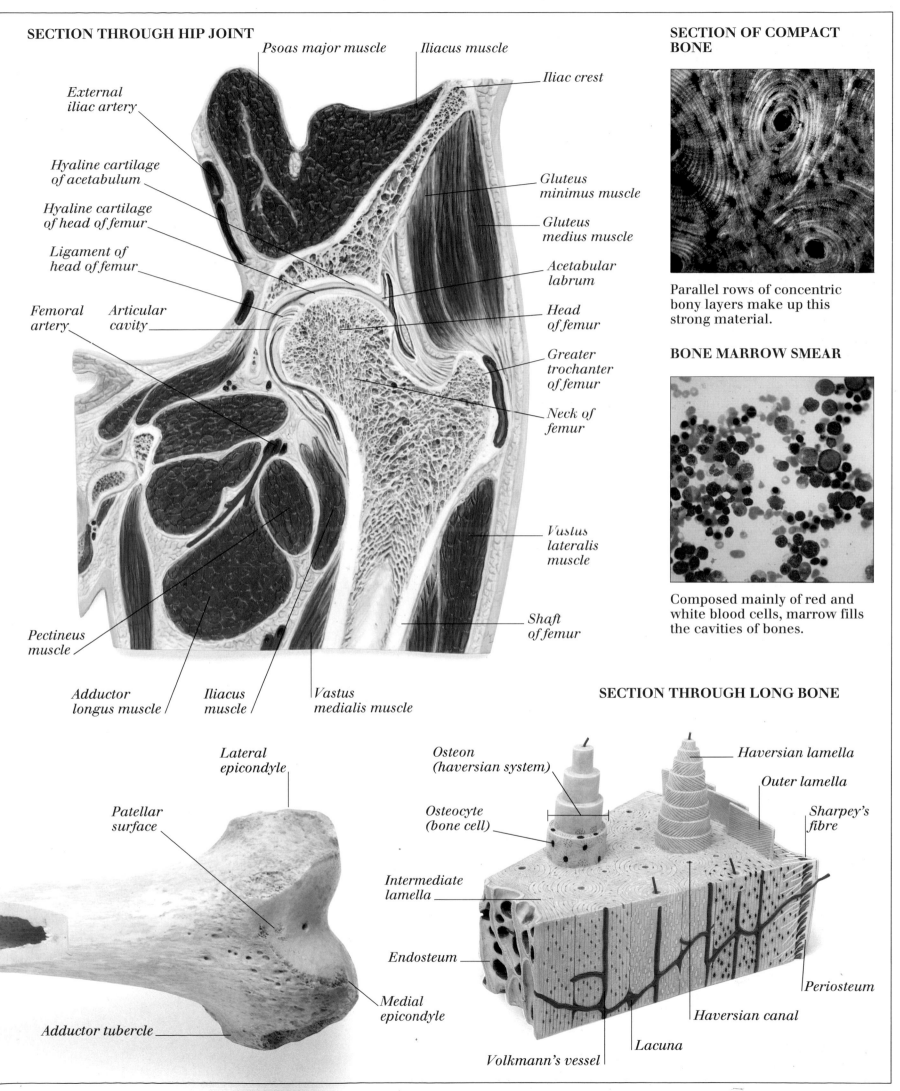

SECTION THROUGH HIP JOINT

Psoas major muscle

Iliacus muscle

Iliac crest

External
iliac artery

Hyaline cartilage
of acetabulum

Hyaline cartilage
of head of femur

Ligament of
head of femur

Femoral
artery

Articular
cavity

Gluteus
minimus muscle

Gluteus
medius muscle

Acetabular
labrum

Head
of femur

Greater
trochanter
of femur

Neck of
femur

Vastus
lateralis
muscle

Shaft
of femur

Pectineus
muscle

Adductor
longus muscle

Iliacus
muscle

Vastus
medialis muscle

SECTION OF COMPACT BONE

Parallel rows of concentric
bony layers make up this
strong material.

BONE MARROW SMEAR

Composed mainly of red and
white blood cells, marrow fills
the cavities of bones.

SECTION THROUGH LONG BONE

Lateral
epicondyle

Patellar
surface

Adductor tubercle

Medial
epicondyle

Osteon
(haversian system)

Osteocyte
(bone cell)

Intermediate
lamella

Endosteum

Volkmann's vessel

Lacuna

Haversian canal

Haversian lamella

Outer lamella

Sharpey's
fibre

Periosteum

21

Muscles 1

THERE ARE THREE MAIN TYPES OF MUSCLE: skeletal muscle (also called voluntary muscle because it can be consciously controlled); smooth muscle (also called involuntary muscle because it is not under voluntary control); and the specialized muscle tissue of the heart. Humans have more than 600 skeletal muscles, which differ in size and shape according to the jobs they do. Skeletal muscles are attached either directly or indirectly (via tendons) to bones, and work in opposing pairs (one muscle in the pair contracts while the other relaxes) to produce body movements as diverse as walking, threading a needle, and an array of facial expressions. Smooth muscles occur in the walls of internal body organs and perform actions such as forcing food through the intestines, contracting the uterus (womb) in childbirth, and pumping blood through the blood vessels.

SOME OTHER MUSCLES IN THE BODY

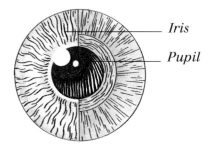

- Iris
- Pupil

IRIS
The muscle fibres contract and dilate (expand) to alter pupil size.

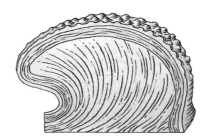

TONGUE
Interlacing layers of muscle allow great mobility.

ILEUM
Opposing muscle layers transport semi-digested food.

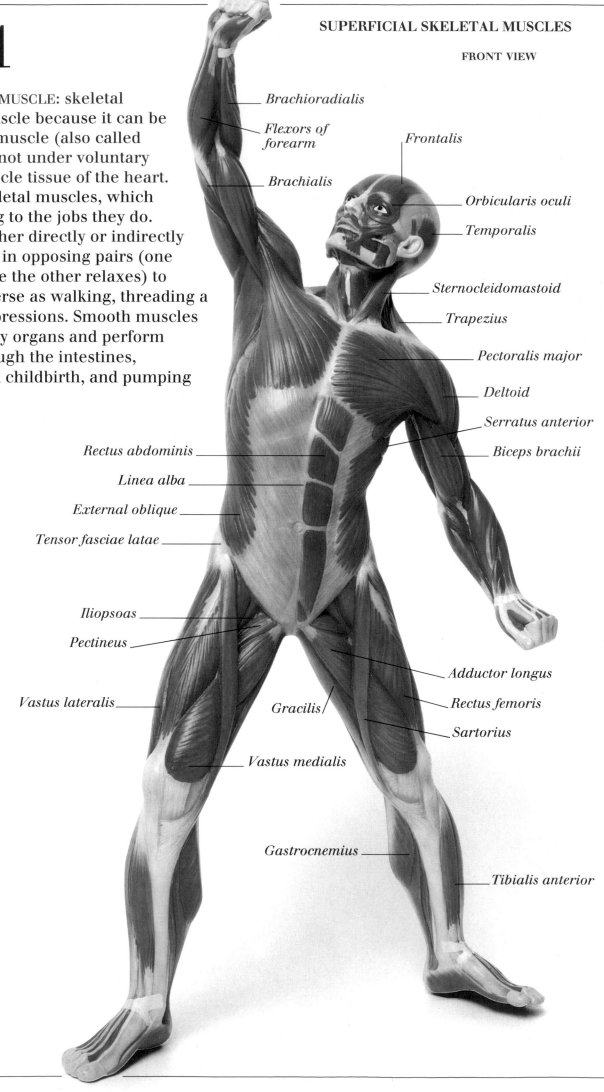

SUPERFICIAL SKELETAL MUSCLES
FRONT VIEW

- Brachioradialis
- Flexors of forearm
- Brachialis
- Frontalis
- Orbicularis oculi
- Temporalis
- Sternocleidomastoid
- Trapezius
- Pectoralis major
- Deltoid
- Serratus anterior
- Biceps brachii
- Rectus abdominis
- Linea alba
- External oblique
- Tensor fasciae latae
- Iliopsoas
- Pectineus
- Adductor longus
- Vastus lateralis
- Gracilis
- Rectus femoris
- Sartorius
- Vastus medialis
- Gastrocnemius
- Tibialis anterior

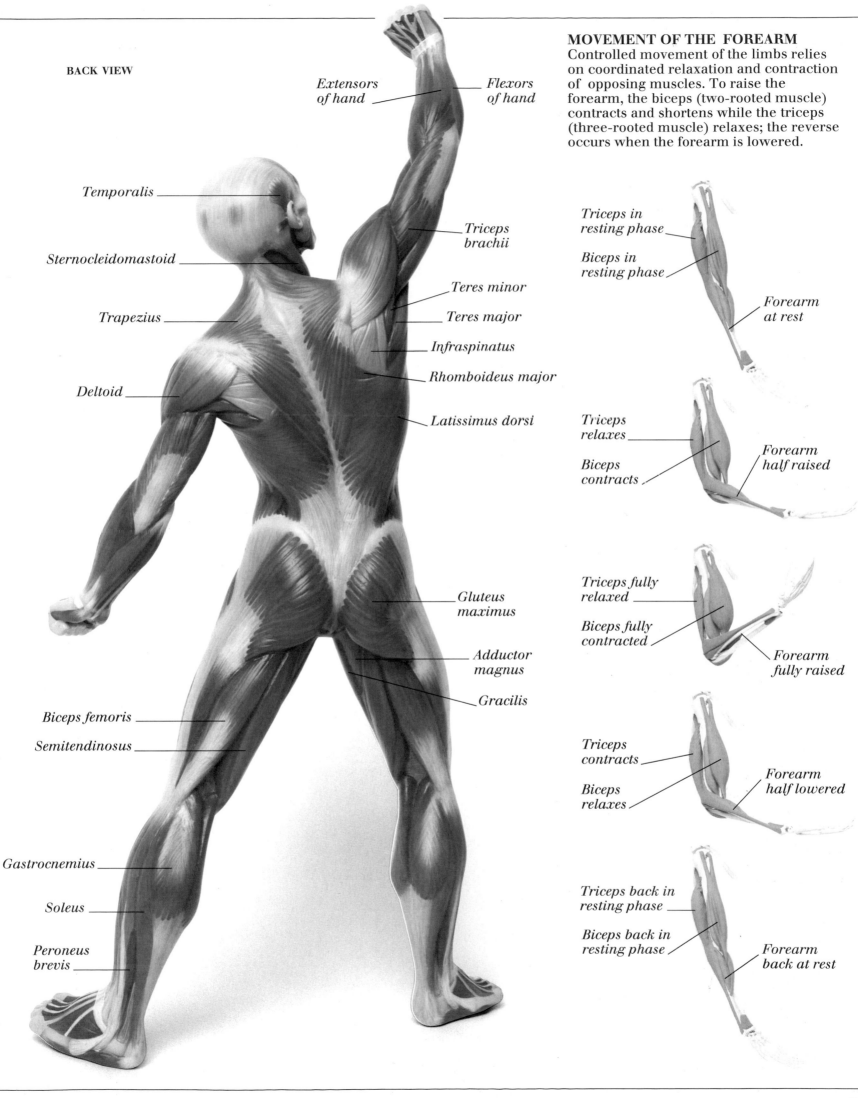

BACK VIEW

Extensors
of hand

Flexors
of hand

Temporalis

Sternocleidomastoid

Trapezius

Deltoid

Triceps
brachii

Teres minor

Teres major

Infraspinatus

Rhomboideus major

Latissimus dorsi

Gluteus
maximus

Adductor
magnus

Gracilis

Biceps femoris

Semitendinosus

Gastrocnemius

Soleus

Peroneus
brevis

MOVEMENT OF THE FOREARM

Controlled movement of the limbs relies on coordinated relaxation and contraction of opposing muscles. To raise the forearm, the biceps (two-rooted muscle) contracts and shortens while the triceps (three-rooted muscle) relaxes; the reverse occurs when the forearm is lowered.

Triceps in
resting phase

Biceps in
resting phase

Forearm
at rest

Triceps
relaxes

Biceps
contracts

Forearm
half raised

Triceps fully
relaxed

Biceps fully
contracted

Forearm
fully raised

Triceps
contracts

Biceps
relaxes

Forearm
half lowered

Triceps back in
resting phase

Biceps back in
resting phase

Forearm
back at rest

Muscles 2

SKELETAL MUSCLE FIBRE

Myofibril

Motor end plate

Synaptic knob

Schwann cell

Motor neuron

Node of Ranvier

Sarcomere

Nucleus

Sarcoplasmic reticulum

Sarcolemma

Endomysium

TYPES OF MUSCLE

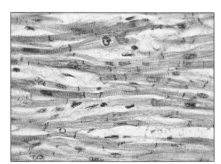

CARDIAC MUSCLE

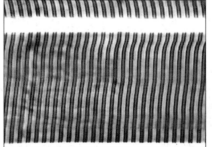

SKELETAL MUSCLE

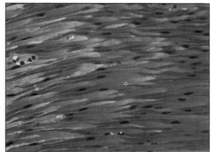

SMOOTH MUSCLE

CONTRACTION OF SKELETAL MUSCLE

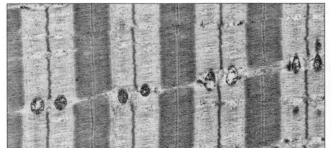

RELAXED STATE

CONTRACTED STATE

MUSCLES OF FACIAL EXPRESSION
A single expression is the result of movement of many muscles; the main muscles of expression are shown in action below.

FRONTALIS

CORRUGATOR SUPERCILII

ORBICULARIS ORIS

ZYGOMATICUS MAJOR

DEPRESSOR ANGULI ORIS

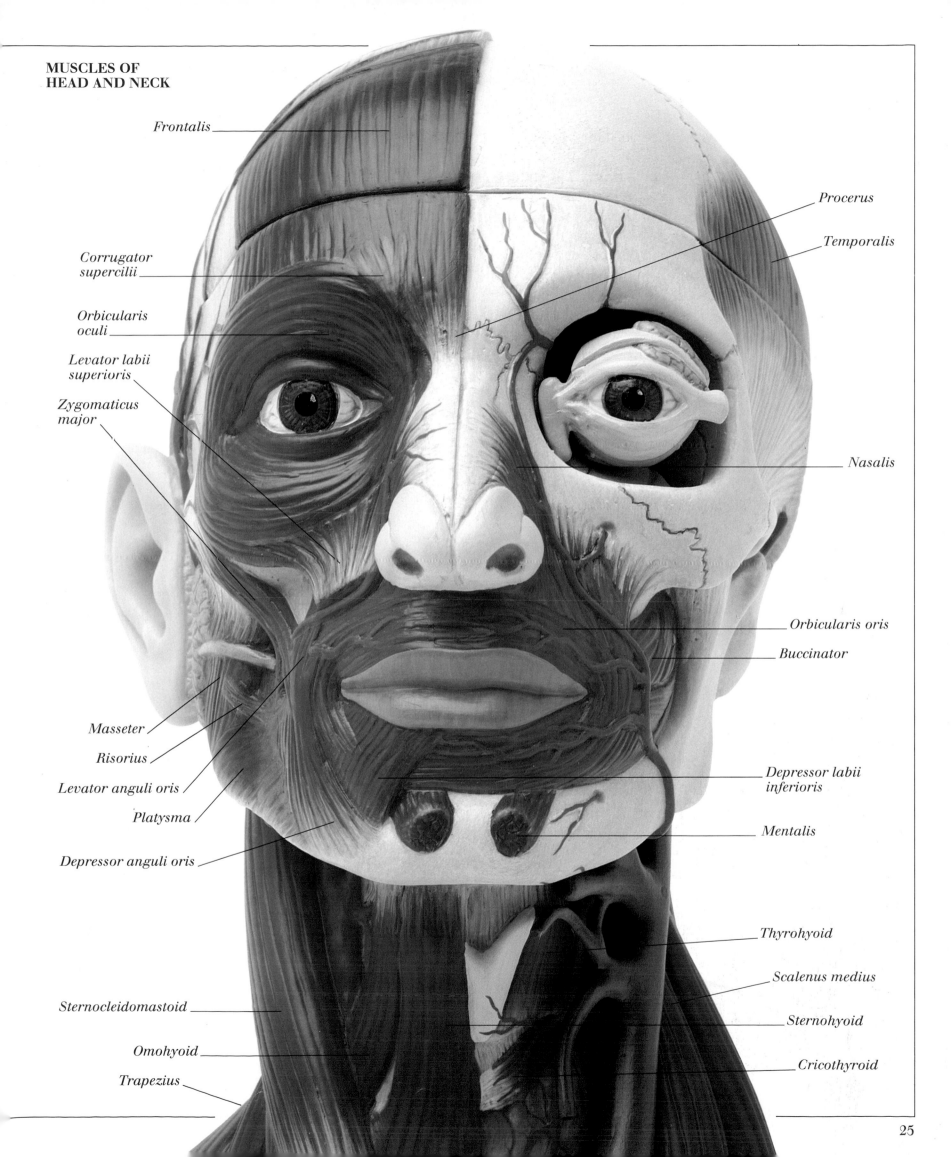

MUSCLES OF HEAD AND NECK

Frontalis

Procerus

Temporalis

Corrugator supercilii

Orbicularis oculi

Levator labii superioris

Zygomaticus major

Nasalis

Orbicularis oris

Buccinator

Masseter

Risorius

Levator anguli oris

Depressor labii inferioris

Platysma

Mentalis

Depressor anguli oris

Thyrohyoid

Scalenus medius

Sternocleidomastoid

Sternohyoid

Omohyoid

Cricothyroid

Trapezius

25

Hands

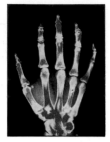

THE HUMAN HAND is an extremely versatile tool, capable of delicate manipulation as well as powerful gripping actions. The arrangement of its 27 small bones, moved by 37 skeletal muscles that are connected to the bones by tendons, allows a wide range of movements. In particular, it is our ability to bring the tips of our thumbs and fingers together, combined with the extraordinary sensitivity of our fingertips due to their rich supply of nerve endings, that gives human hands their unique dexterity.

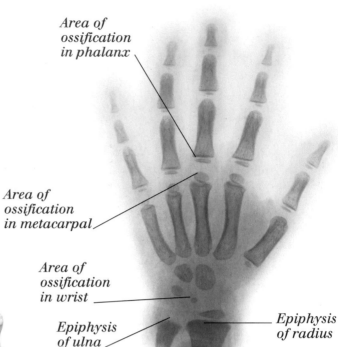

Area of ossification in phalanx

Area of ossification in metacarpal

Area of ossification in wrist

Epiphysis of ulna

Epiphysis of radius

Areas of cartilage in the wrist and at the ends of the finger bones are the sites of growth and have still to ossify.

BONES OF HAND

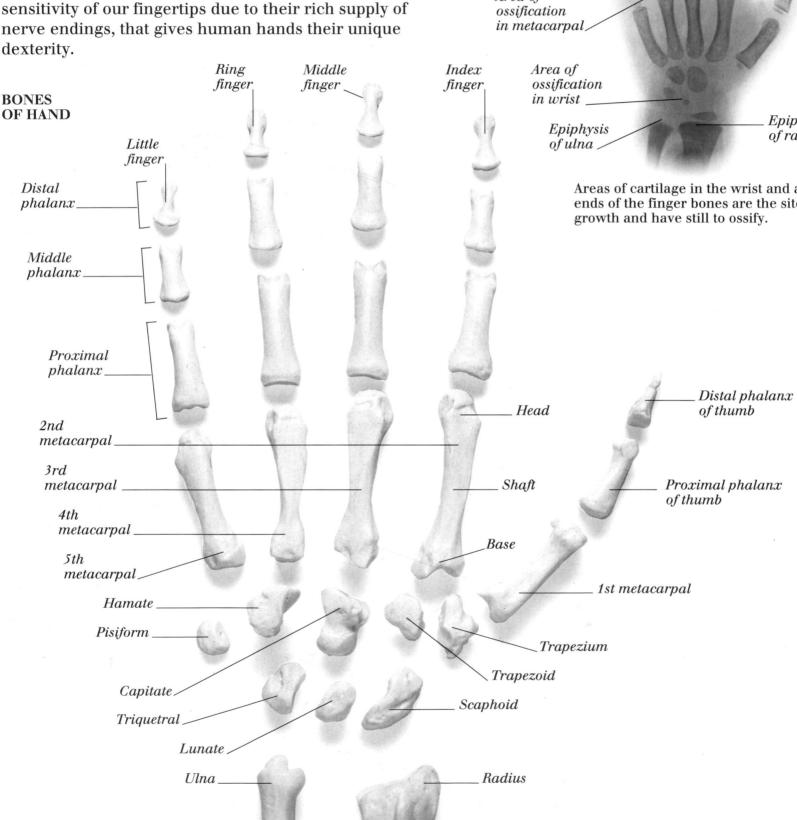

Ring finger

Middle finger

Index finger

Little finger

Distal phalanx

Middle phalanx

Proximal phalanx

2nd metacarpal

3rd metacarpal

4th metacarpal

5th metacarpal

Hamate

Pisiform

Capitate

Triquetral

Lunate

Ulna

Head

Shaft

Base

Distal phalanx of thumb

Proximal phalanx of thumb

1st metacarpal

Trapezium

Trapezoid

Scaphoid

Radius

STRUCTURES UNDERLYING SKIN OF PALM OF HAND

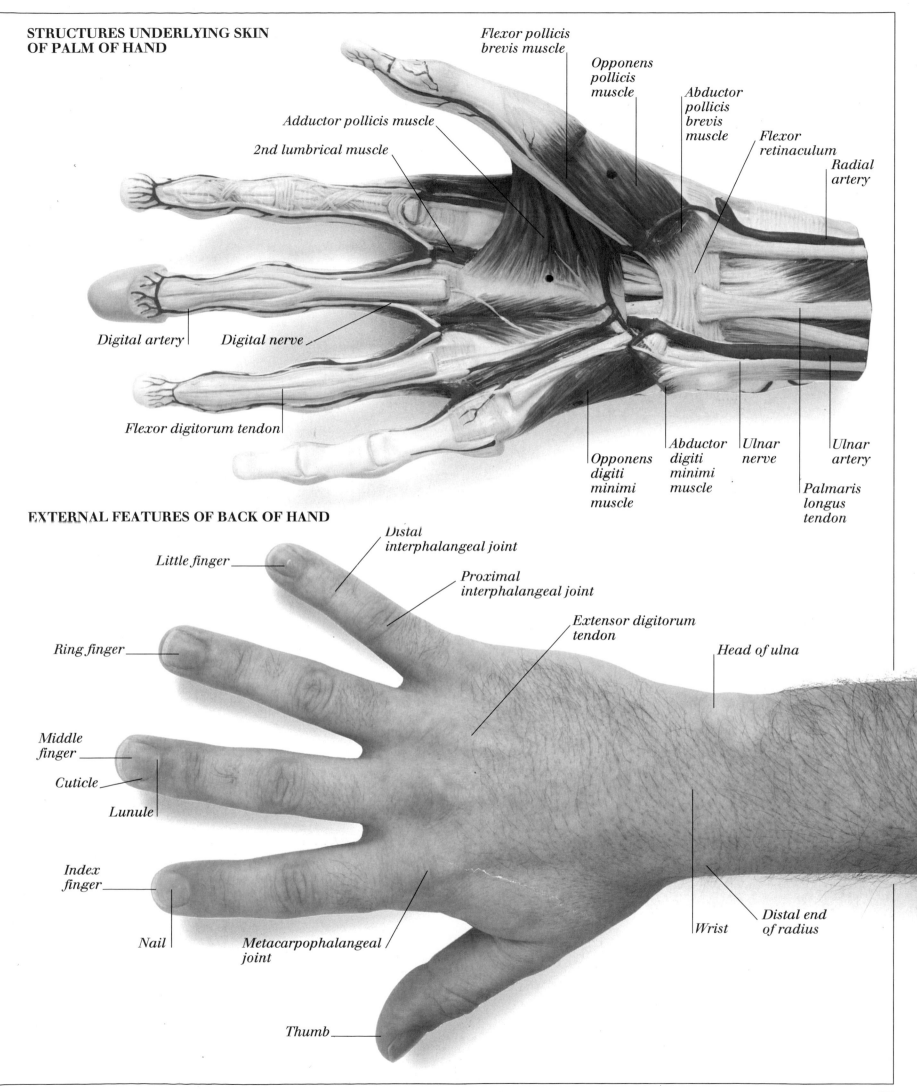

Flexor pollicis brevis muscle

Opponens pollicis muscle

Abductor pollicis brevis muscle

Flexor retinaculum

Radial artery

Adductor pollicis muscle

2nd lumbrical muscle

Digital artery

Digital nerve

Flexor digitorum tendon

Opponens digiti minimi muscle

Abductor digiti minimi muscle

Ulnar nerve

Ulnar artery

Palmaris longus tendon

EXTERNAL FEATURES OF BACK OF HAND

Distal interphalangeal joint

Little finger

Proximal interphalangeal joint

Extensor digitorum tendon

Head of ulna

Ring finger

Middle finger

Cuticle

Lunule

Index finger

Nail

Metacarpophalangeal joint

Wrist

Distal end of radius

Thumb

27

Feet

THE FEET AND TOES are essential elements in body movement. They bear and propel the weight of the body during walking and running, and also help to maintain balance during changes of body position. Each foot has 26 bones, more than 100 ligaments, and 33 muscles, some of which are attached to the lower leg. The heel pad and the arch of the foot act as shock absorbers, providing a cushion against the jolts that occur with every step.

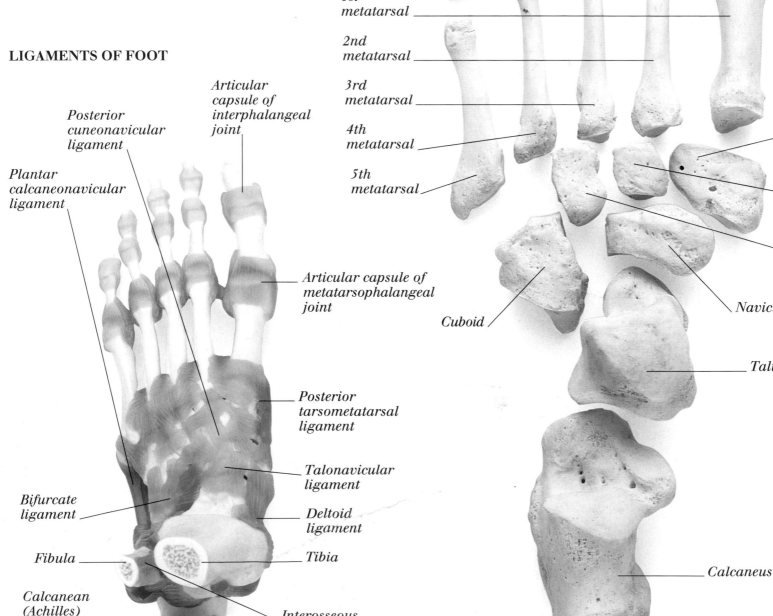

LIGAMENTS OF FOOT

2nd toe

Hallux (big toe)

3rd toe

Distal phalanx of hallux

4th toe

5th (little) toe

Proximal phalanx of hallux

Distal phalanx

Middle phalanx

Proximal phalanx

1st metatarsal

2nd metatarsal

3rd metatarsal

4th metatarsal

5th metatarsal

1st cuneiform

2nd cuneiform

3rd cuneiform

Navicular

Cuboid

Talus

Calcaneus

Articular capsule of interphalangeal joint

Posterior cuneonavicular ligament

Plantar calcaneonavicular ligament

Articular capsule of metatarsophalangeal joint

Posterior tarsometatarsal ligament

Talonavicular ligament

Deltoid ligament

Bifurcate ligament

Fibula

Tibia

Calcanean (Achilles) tendon

Interosseous ligament

STRUCTURES UNDERLYING SKIN OF FOOT

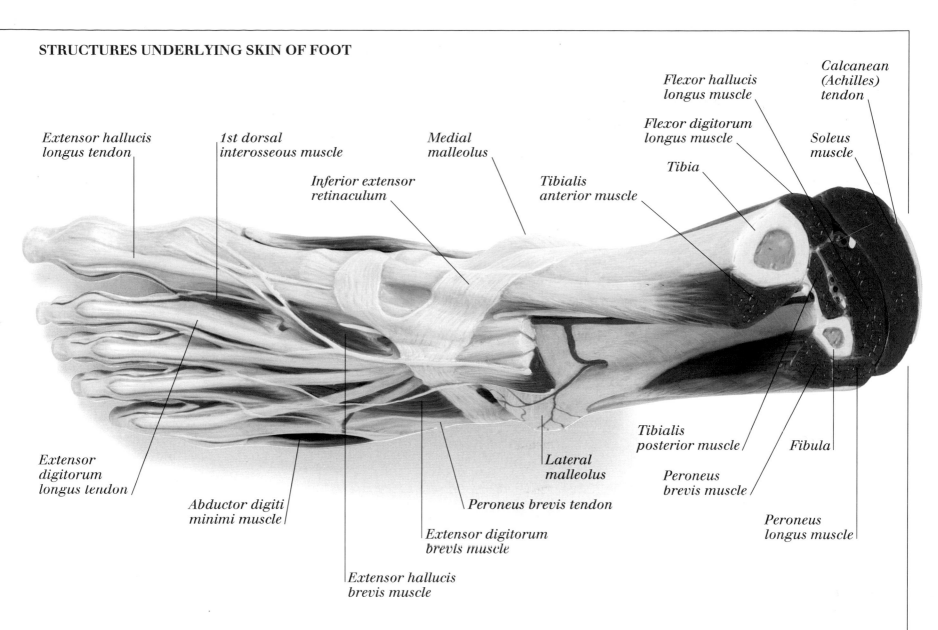

Extensor hallucis longus tendon

1st dorsal interosseous muscle

Inferior extensor retinaculum

Medial malleolus

Tibialis anterior muscle

Tibia

Flexor hallucis longus muscle

Flexor digitorum longus muscle

Soleus muscle

Calcanean (Achilles) tendon

Extensor digitorum longus tendon

Abductor digiti minimi muscle

Extensor hallucis brevis muscle

Extensor digitorum brevis muscle

Peroneus brevis tendon

Lateral malleolus

Tibialis posterior muscle

Peroneus brevis muscle

Fibula

Peroneus longus muscle

EXTERNAL FEATURES OF FOOT

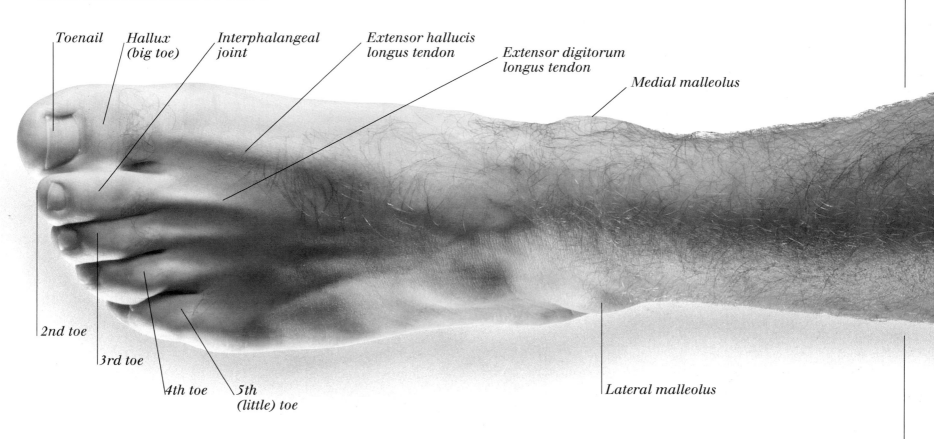

Toenail

Hallux (big toe)

Interphalangeal joint

Extensor hallucis longus tendon

Extensor digitorum longus tendon

Medial malleolus

2nd toe

3rd toe

4th toe

5th (little) toe

Lateral malleolus

Skin and hair

SKIN IS THE BODY'S LARGEST ORGAN, a waterproof barrier that protects the internal organs against infection, injury, and harmful sun rays. The skin is also an important sensory organ and helps to control body temperature. The outer layer of the skin, known as the epidermis, is coated with keratin, a tough, horny protein that is also the chief consistituent of hair and nails. Dead cells are shed from the skin's surface and are replaced by new cells from the base of the epidermis, the region that also produces the skin pigment, melanin. The dermis contains most of the skin's living structures, and includes nerve endings, blood vessels, elastic fibres, sweat glands that cool the skin, and sebaceous glands that produce oil to keep the skin supple. Beneath the dermis lies the subcutaneous tissue (hypodermis), which is rich in fat and blood vessels. Hair shafts grow from hair follicles situated in the dermis and subcutaneous tissue. Hair grows on every part of the skin apart from the palms of the hands and soles of the feet.

SECTION OF HAIR

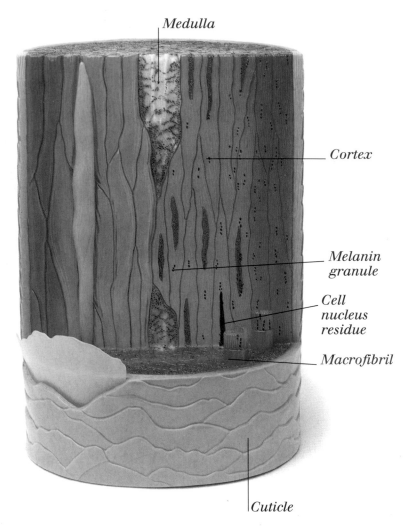

Medulla

Cortex

Melanin granule

Cell nucleus residue

Macrofibril

Cuticle

SECTIONS OF DIFFERENT TYPES OF SKIN

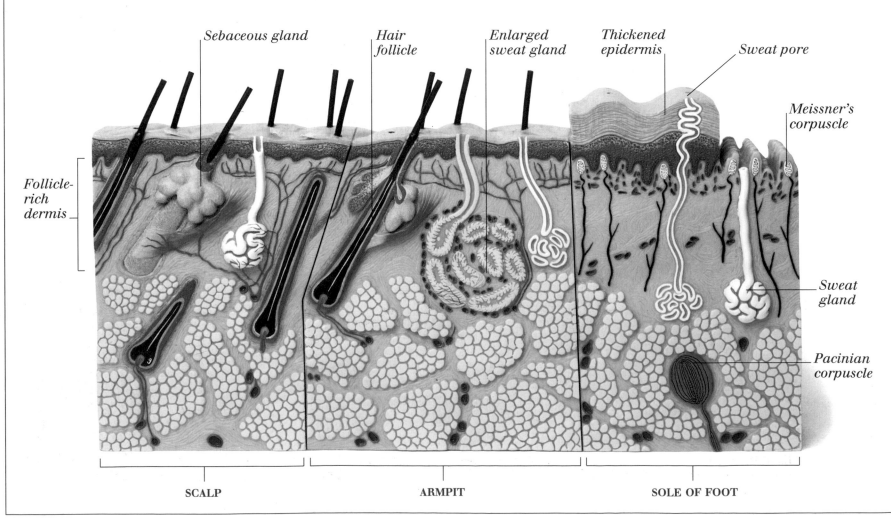

Sebaceous gland

Hair follicle

Enlarged sweat gland

Thickened epidermis

Sweat pore

Meissner's corpuscle

Follicle-rich dermis

Sweat gland

Pacinian corpuscle

SCALP

ARMPIT

SOLE OF FOOT

SECTION OF SKIN

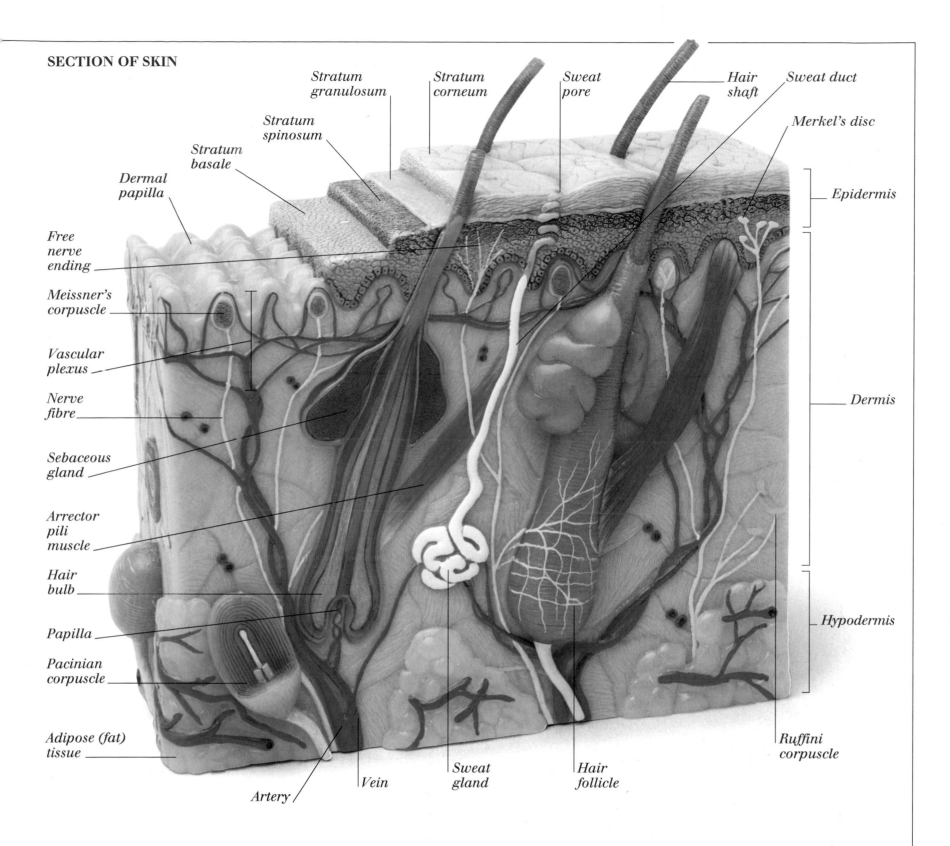

Stratum granulosum

Stratum corneum

Sweat pore

Hair shaft

Sweat duct

Stratum spinosum

Merkel's disc

Stratum basale

Dermal papilla

Epidermis

Free nerve ending

Meissner's corpuscle

Vascular plexus

Nerve fibre

Dermis

Sebaceous gland

Arrector pili muscle

Hair bulb

Papilla

Hypodermis

Pacinian corpuscle

Adipose (fat) tissue

Ruffini corpuscle

Artery

Vein

Sweat gland

Hair follicle

PHOTOMICROGRAPHS OF SKIN AND HAIR

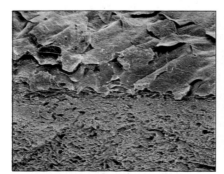

SECTION OF SKIN
The flaky cells at the skin's surface are shed continuously.

SWEAT PORE
This allows loss of fluid as part of temperature control.

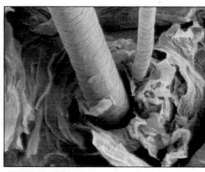

SKIN HAIR
Two hairs pushing through the outer layer of skin.

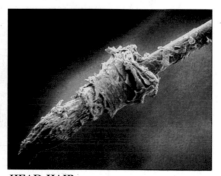

HEAD HAIR
The root and part of the shaft of a hair from the scalp.

Brain

THE BRAIN IS THE MAJOR ORGAN of the central nervous system and the control centre for all the body's voluntary and involuntary activities. It is also responsible for the complexities of thought, memory, emotion, and language. In adults, this complex organ is a mere 1.4 kg (3 lb) in weight, containing over 10 thousand million nerve cells. Three distinct regions can easily be seen – the brainstem, the cerebellum, and the large cerebrum. The brainstem controls vital body functions, such as breathing and digestion. The cerebellum's main functions are the maintenance of posture and the coordination of body movements. The cerebrum, which consists of the right and left cerebral hemispheres joined by the corpus callosum, is the site of most conscious and intelligent activities.

MRI SCAN OF TRANSVERSE SECTION THROUGH BRAIN

White matter

Skull

Scalp

Grey matter

Lateral ventricle

Longitudinal fissure

Coronal section

Sagittal section

SAGITTAL SECTION THROUGH BRAIN

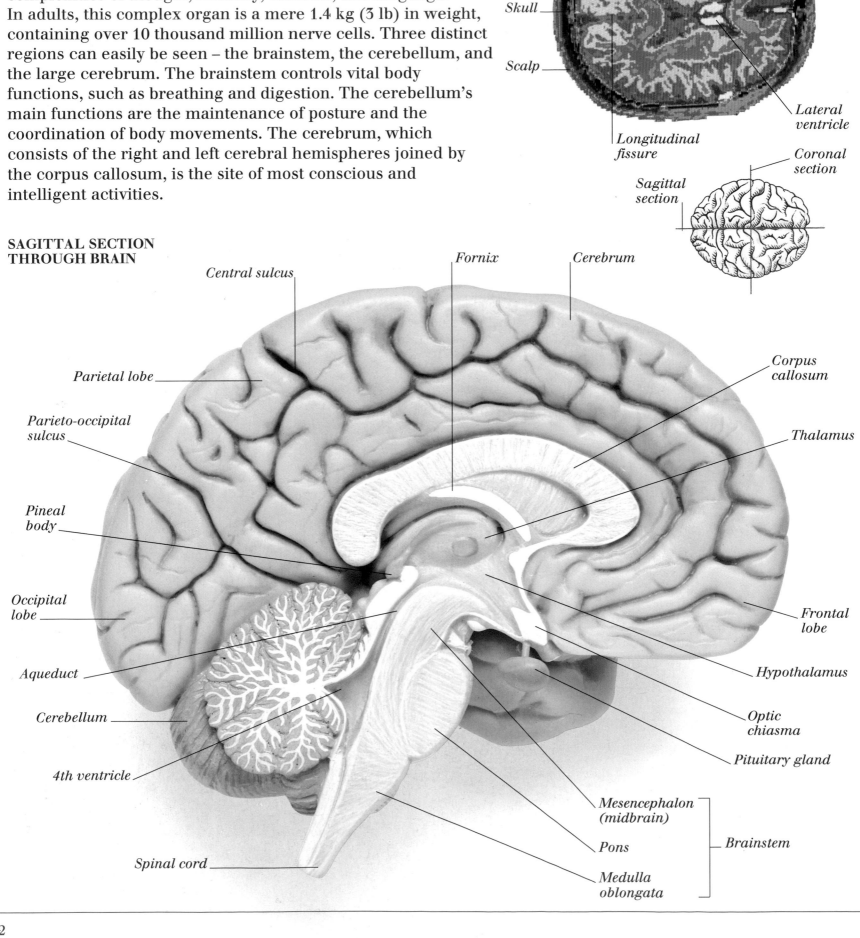

Central sulcus

Fornix

Cerebrum

Parietal lobe

Parieto-occipital sulcus

Corpus callosum

Thalamus

Pineal body

Occipital lobe

Aqueduct

Cerebellum

Frontal lobe

Hypothalamus

Optic chiasma

Pituitary gland

4th ventricle

Spinal cord

Mesencephalon (midbrain)

Pons

Medulla oblongata

Brainstem

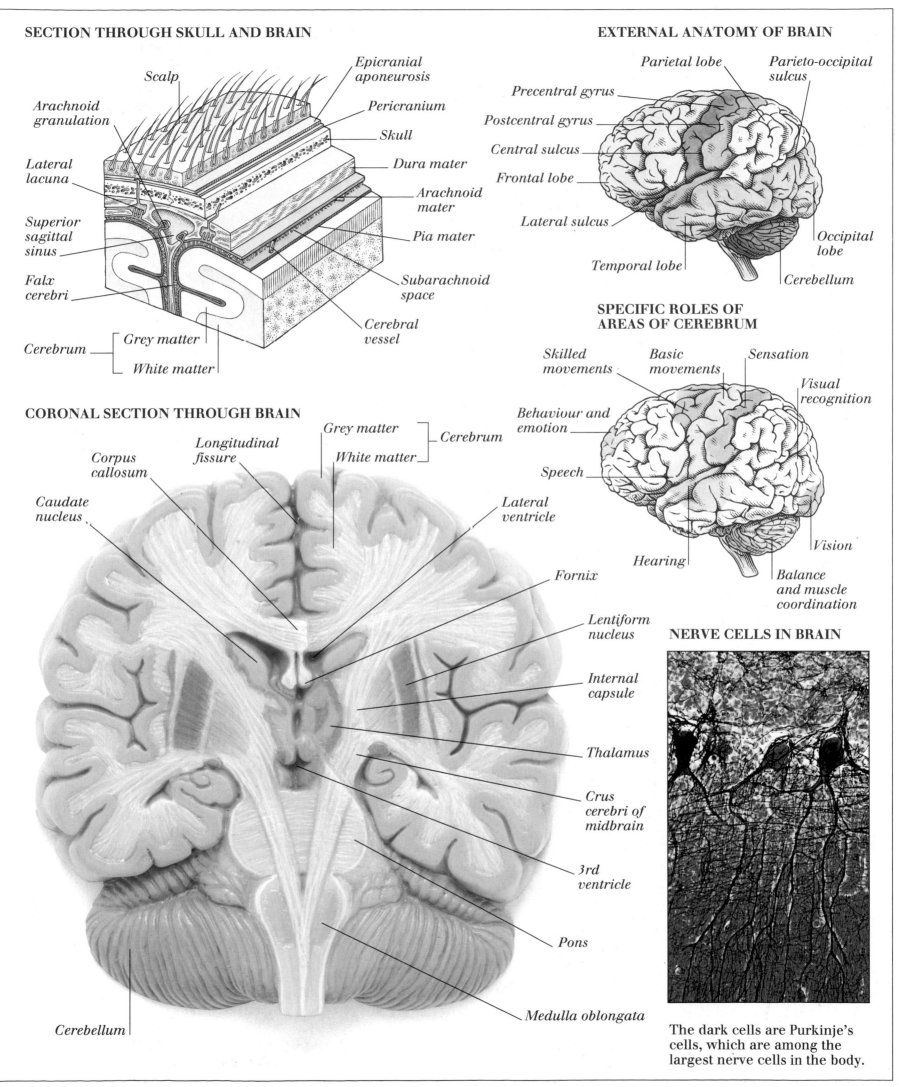

SECTION THROUGH SKULL AND BRAIN

Scalp

Epicranial aponeurosis

Arachnoid granulation

Pericranium

Skull

Lateral lacuna

Dura mater

Arachnoid mater

Superior sagittal sinus

Pia mater

Falx cerebri

Subarachnoid space

Cerebral vessel

Cerebrum — Grey matter / White matter

EXTERNAL ANATOMY OF BRAIN

Parietal lobe

Parieto-occipital sulcus

Precentral gyrus

Postcentral gyrus

Central sulcus

Frontal lobe

Lateral sulcus

Occipital lobe

Temporal lobe

Cerebellum

SPECIFIC ROLES OF AREAS OF CEREBRUM

Skilled movements

Basic movements

Sensation

Visual recognition

Behaviour and emotion

Speech

Hearing

Vision

Balance and muscle coordination

CORONAL SECTION THROUGH BRAIN

Grey matter

White matter

Cerebrum

Corpus callosum

Longitudinal fissure

Caudate nucleus

Lateral ventricle

Fornix

Lentiform nucleus

Internal capsule

Thalamus

Crus cerebri of midbrain

3rd ventricle

Pons

Medulla oblongata

Cerebellum

NERVE CELLS IN BRAIN

The dark cells are Purkinje's cells, which are among the largest nerve cells in the body.

Nervous system

THE NERVOUS SYSTEM IS THE BODY'S internal, electrochemical, communications network. Its main parts are the brain, spinal cord, and nerves. The brain and spinal cord form the central nervous system (CNS), the body's chief controlling and coordinating centres. Billions of long neurons, many grouped as nerves, make up the peripheral nervous system, transmitting nerve impulses between the CNS and other regions of the body. Each neuron has three parts: a cell body, branching dendrites that receive chemical signals from other neurons, and a tube-like axon that conveys these signals as electrical impulses.

CENTRAL AND PERIPHERAL NERVOUS SYSTEMS

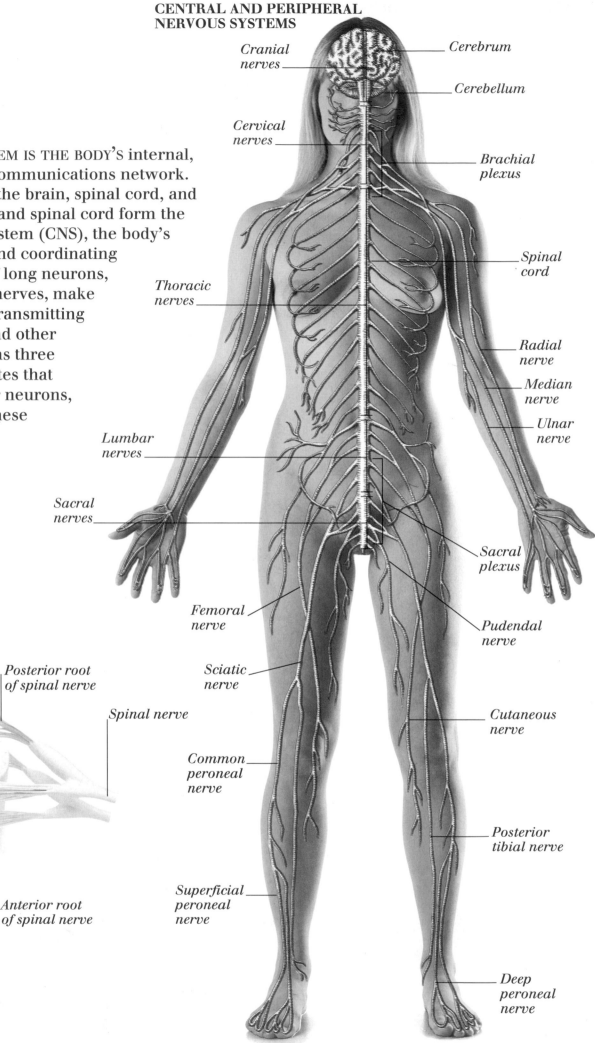

- Cranial nerves
- Cerebrum
- Cerebellum
- Cervical nerves
- Brachial plexus
- Thoracic nerves
- Spinal cord
- Radial nerve
- Median nerve
- Ulnar nerve
- Lumbar nerves
- Sacral nerves
- Sacral plexus
- Femoral nerve
- Pudendal nerve
- Sciatic nerve
- Cutaneous nerve
- Common peroneal nerve
- Posterior tibial nerve
- Superficial peroneal nerve
- Deep peroneal nerve

SECTION THROUGH SPINAL CORD

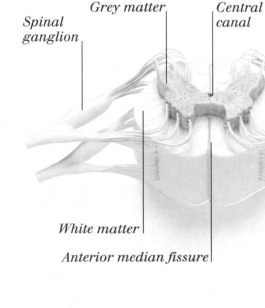

- Spinal ganglion
- Grey matter
- Central canal
- Posterior root of spinal nerve
- Spinal nerve
- White matter
- Anterior median fissure
- Anterior root of spinal nerve

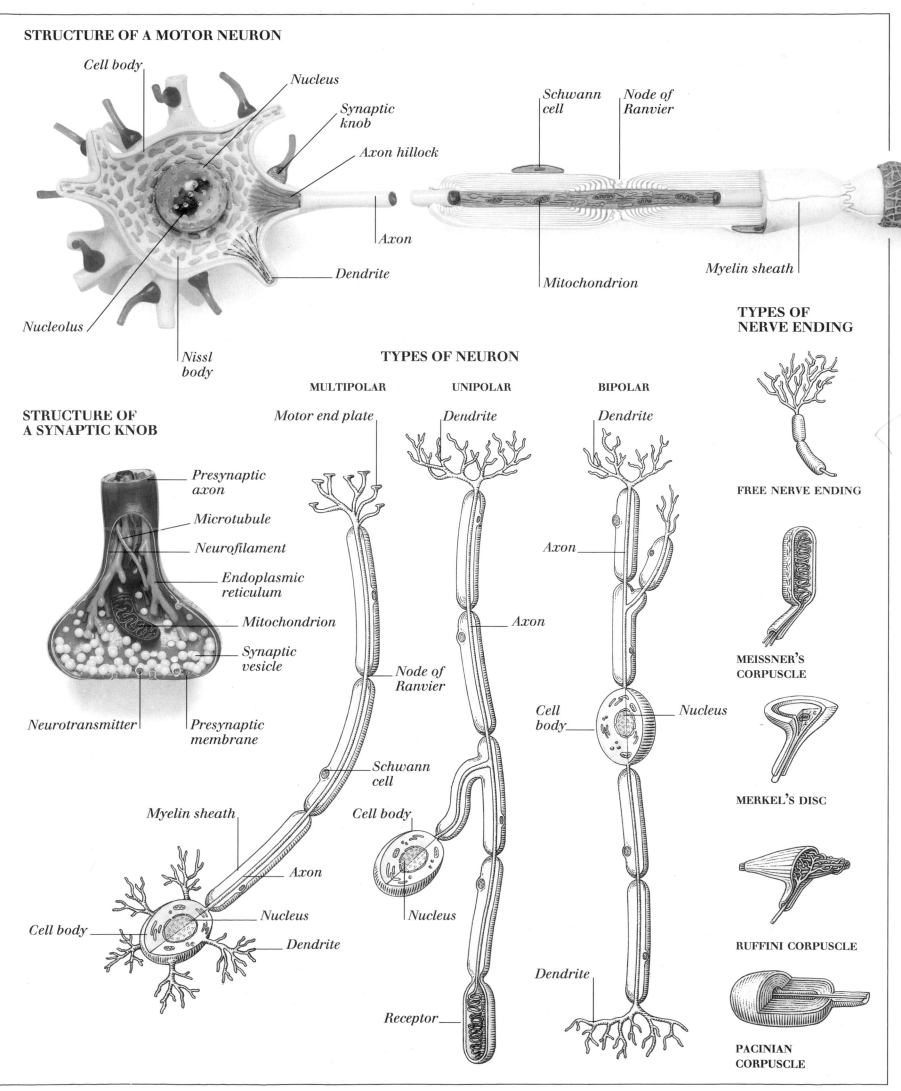

STRUCTURE OF A MOTOR NEURON

Cell body

Nucleus

Synaptic knob

Axon hillock

Axon

Dendrite

Nucleolus

Nissl body

Schwann cell

Node of Ranvier

Mitochondrion

Myelin sheath

TYPES OF NERVE ENDING

FREE NERVE ENDING

MEISSNER'S CORPUSCLE

MERKEL'S DISC

RUFFINI CORPUSCLE

PACINIAN CORPUSCLE

STRUCTURE OF A SYNAPTIC KNOB

Presynaptic axon

Microtubule

Neurofilament

Endoplasmic reticulum

Mitochondrion

Synaptic vesicle

Neurotransmitter

Presynaptic membrane

TYPES OF NEURON

MULTIPOLAR

Motor end plate

Node of Ranvier

Schwann cell

Myelin sheath

Axon

Cell body

Nucleus

Dendrite

UNIPOLAR

Dendrite

Axon

Cell body

Nucleus

Receptor

BIPOLAR

Dendrite

Axon

Cell body

Nucleus

Dendrite

35

Eye

THE EYE IS THE ORGAN OF SIGHT. The two eyeballs, protected within bony sockets called orbits and on the outside by the eyelids, eyebrows, and tear film, are directly connected to the brain by the optic nerves. Each eye is moved by six muscles, which are attached around the eyeball. Light rays entering the eye through the pupil are focused by the cornea and lens to form an image on the retina. The retina contains millions of light-sensitive cells, called rods and cones, which convert the image into a pattern of nerve impulses. These impulses are transmitted along the optic nerve to the brain. Information from the two optic nerves is processed in the brain to produce a single coordinated image.

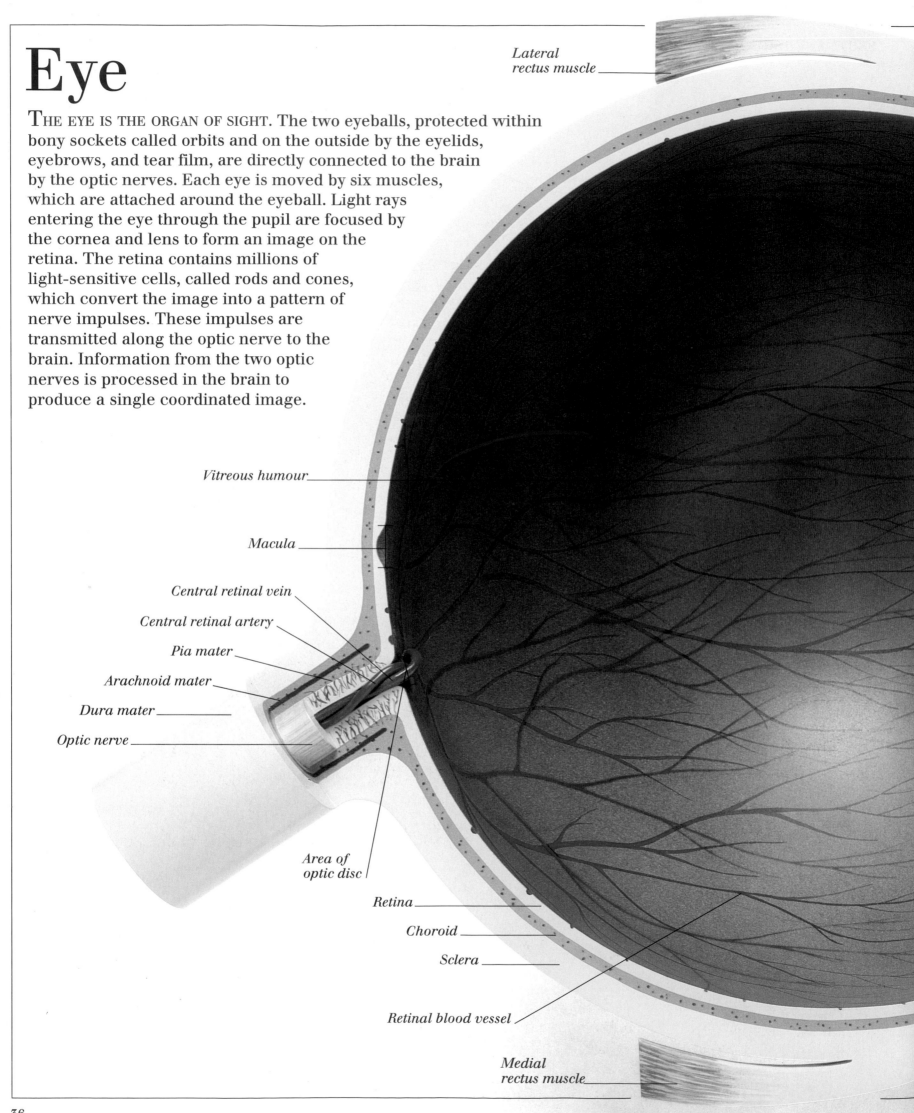

Lateral rectus muscle

Vitreous humour

Macula

Central retinal vein

Central retinal artery

Pia mater

Arachnoid mater

Dura mater

Optic nerve

Area of optic disc

Retina

Choroid

Sclera

Retinal blood vessel

Medial rectus muscle

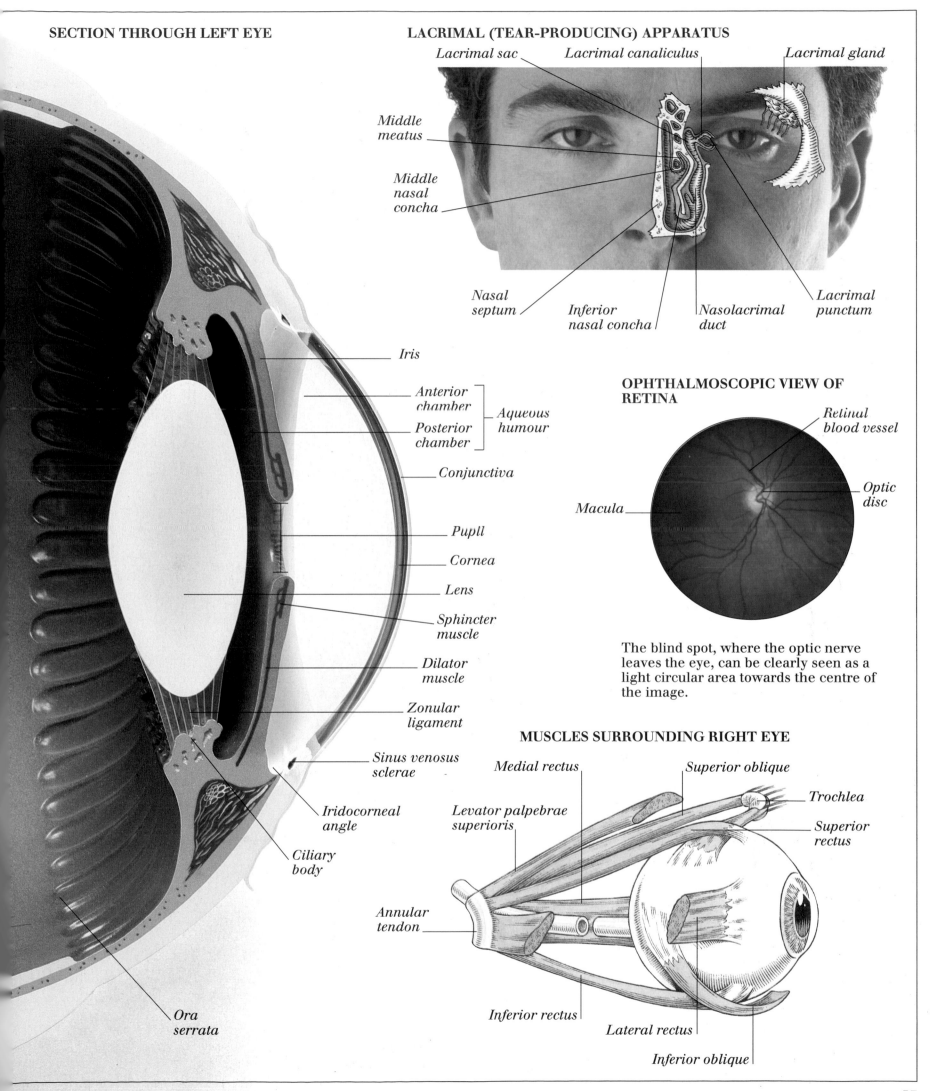

SECTION THROUGH LEFT EYE

Iris

Anterior chamber
Posterior chamber
} Aqueous humour

Conjunctiva

Pupil

Cornea

Lens

Sphincter muscle

Dilator muscle

Zonular ligament

Sinus venosus sclerae

Iridocorneal angle

Ciliary body

Ora serrata

LACRIMAL (TEAR-PRODUCING) APPARATUS

Lacrimal sac

Lacrimal canaliculus

Lacrimal gland

Middle meatus

Middle nasal concha

Nasal septum

Inferior nasal concha

Nasolacrimal duct

Lacrimal punctum

OPHTHALMOSCOPIC VIEW OF RETINA

Retinal blood vessel

Optic disc

Macula

The blind spot, where the optic nerve leaves the eye, can be clearly seen as a light circular area towards the centre of the image.

MUSCLES SURROUNDING RIGHT EYE

Medial rectus

Superior oblique

Trochlea

Levator palpebrae superioris

Superior rectus

Annular tendon

Inferior rectus

Lateral rectus

Inferior oblique

Ear

THE EAR IS THE ORGAN OF HEARING AND BALANCE. The outer ear consists of a flap called the auricle or pinna and the auditory canal. The main functional parts – the middle and inner ears – are enclosed within the skull. The middle ear consists of three tiny bones, known as auditory ossicles, and the eustachian tube, which links the ear to the back of the nose. The inner ear consists of the spiral-shaped cochlea, and also the semicircular canals and the vestibule, which are the organs of balance. Sound waves entering the ear travel through the auditory canal to the tympanic membrane (eardrum), where they are converted to vibrations that are transmitted via the ossicles to the cochlea. Here, the vibrations are converted by millions of microscopic hairs into electrical nerve signals to be interpreted by the brain.

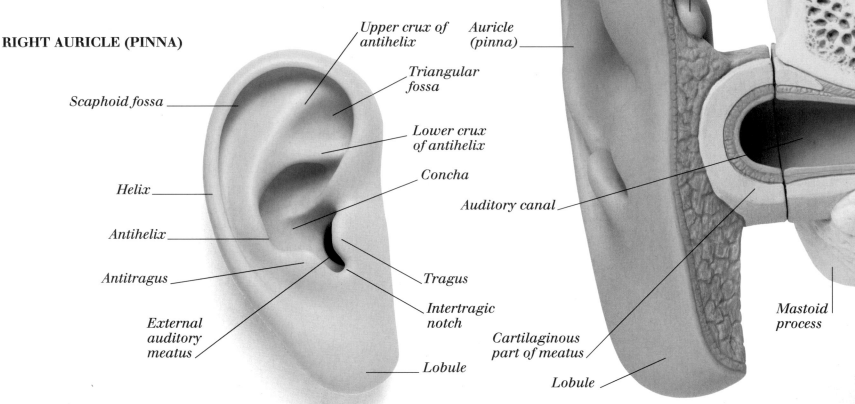

RIGHT AURICLE (PINNA)

- Upper crux of antihelix
- Auricle (pinna)
- Triangular fossa
- Scaphoid fossa
- Lower crux of antihelix
- Helix
- Concha
- Antihelix
- Auditory canal
- Antitragus
- Tragus
- Intertragic notch
- External auditory meatus
- Cartilaginous part of meatus
- Lobule
- Temporal bone
- Cartilage of auricle
- Mastoid process
- Lobule

OSSICLES OF MIDDLE EAR

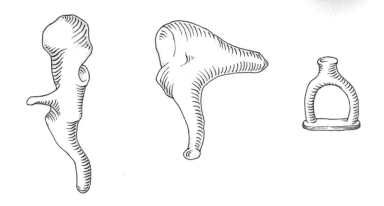

MALLEUS (HAMMER) **INCUS (ANVIL)** **STAPES (STIRRUP)**

These three tiny bones connect to form a bridge between the tympanic membrane and the oval window. With a system of membranes they convey sound vibrations to the inner ear.

INTERNAL STRUCTURE OF AMPULLA

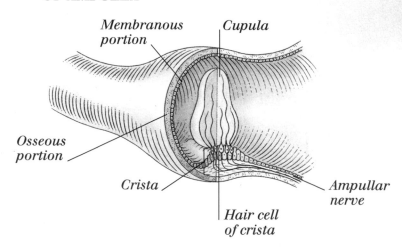

- Membranous portion
- Cupula
- Osseous portion
- Crista
- Hair cell of crista
- Ampullar nerve

LABYRINTH

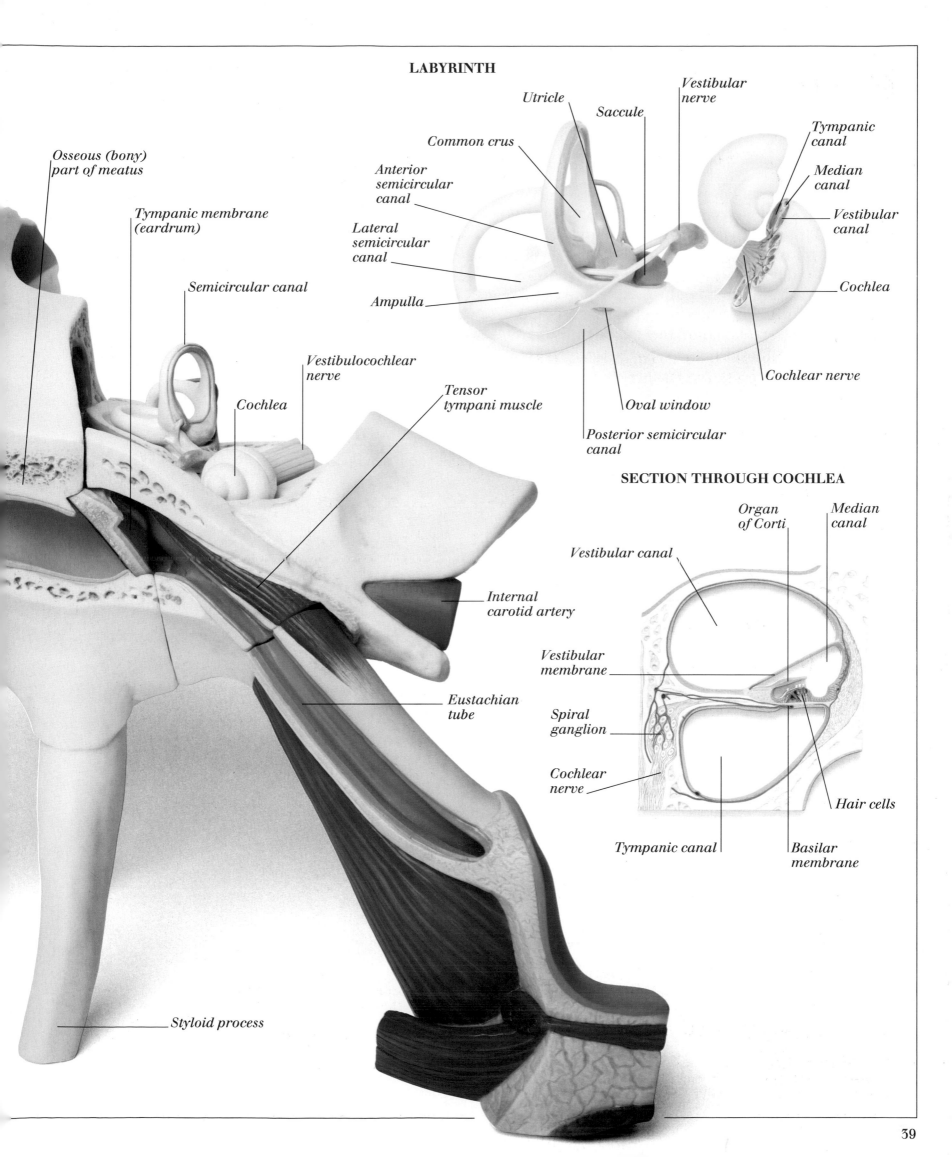

Utricle

Saccule

Vestibular nerve

Common crus

Tympanic canal

Anterior semicircular canal

Median canal

Lateral semicircular canal

Vestibular canal

Osseous (bony) part of meatus

Tympanic membrane (eardrum)

Cochlea

Semicircular canal

Ampulla

Vestibulocochlear nerve

Cochlea

Tensor tympani muscle

Cochlear nerve

Oval window

Posterior semicircular canal

Internal carotid artery

SECTION THROUGH COCHLEA

Organ of Corti

Median canal

Vestibular canal

Vestibular membrane

Spiral ganglion

Cochlear nerve

Tympanic canal

Basilar membrane

Hair cells

Eustachian tube

Styloid process

Nose, mouth, and throat

WITH EVERY BREATH, air passes through the nasal cavity down the pharynx (throat), larynx ("voice box"), and trachea (windpipe) to the lungs. The nasal cavity warms and moistens air, and the tiny layers in its lining protect the airway against damage by foreign bodies. During swallowing, the tongue moves up and back, the larynx rises, the epiglottis closes off the entrance to the trachea, and the soft palate separates the nasal cavity from the pharynx. Saliva, secreted from three pairs of salivary glands, lubricates food to make swallowing easier; it also begins the chemical breakdown of food, and helps to produce taste. The senses of taste and smell are closely linked. Both depend on the detection of dissolved molecules by sensory receptors in the olfactory nerve endings of the nose and in the taste buds of the tongue.

STRUCTURE OF TONGUE

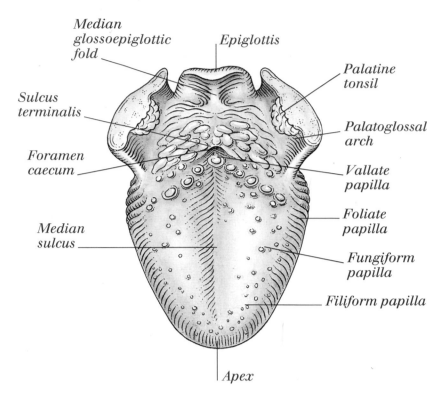

Median glossoepiglottic fold
Epiglottis
Palatine tonsil
Sulcus terminalis
Palatoglossal arch
Foramen caecum
Vallate papilla
Foliate papilla
Median sulcus
Fungiform papilla
Filiform papilla
Apex

TASTE AREAS ON TONGUE

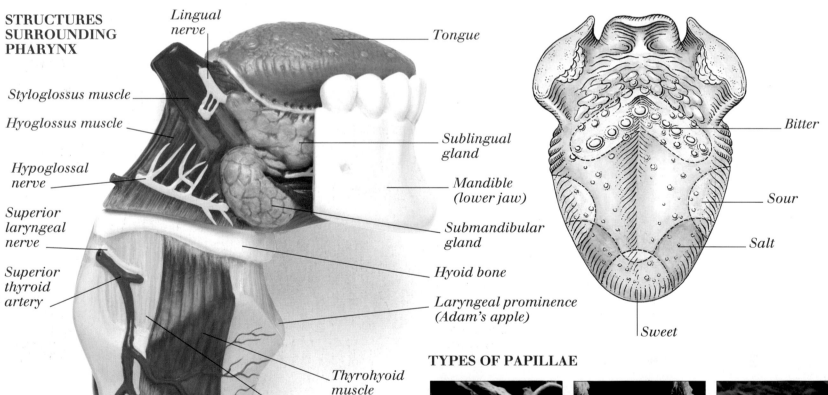

STRUCTURES SURROUNDING PHARYNX

Lingual nerve
Tongue
Styloglossus muscle
Hyoglossus muscle
Sublingual gland
Hypoglossal nerve
Mandible (lower jaw)
Superior laryngeal nerve
Submandibular gland
Superior thyroid artery
Hyoid bone
Laryngeal prominence (Adam's apple)
Thyrohyoid muscle
Thyrohyoid membrane
Cricothyroid muscle
Cricothyroid ligament
Thyroid gland
Trachea

Bitter
Sour
Salt
Sweet

TYPES OF PAPILLAE

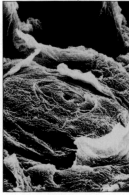

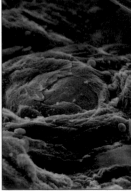

FILIFORM PAPILLAE   **FUNGIFORM PAPILLAE**   **VALLATE PAPILLAE**

SECTION THROUGH NOSE, MOUTH, AND THROAT

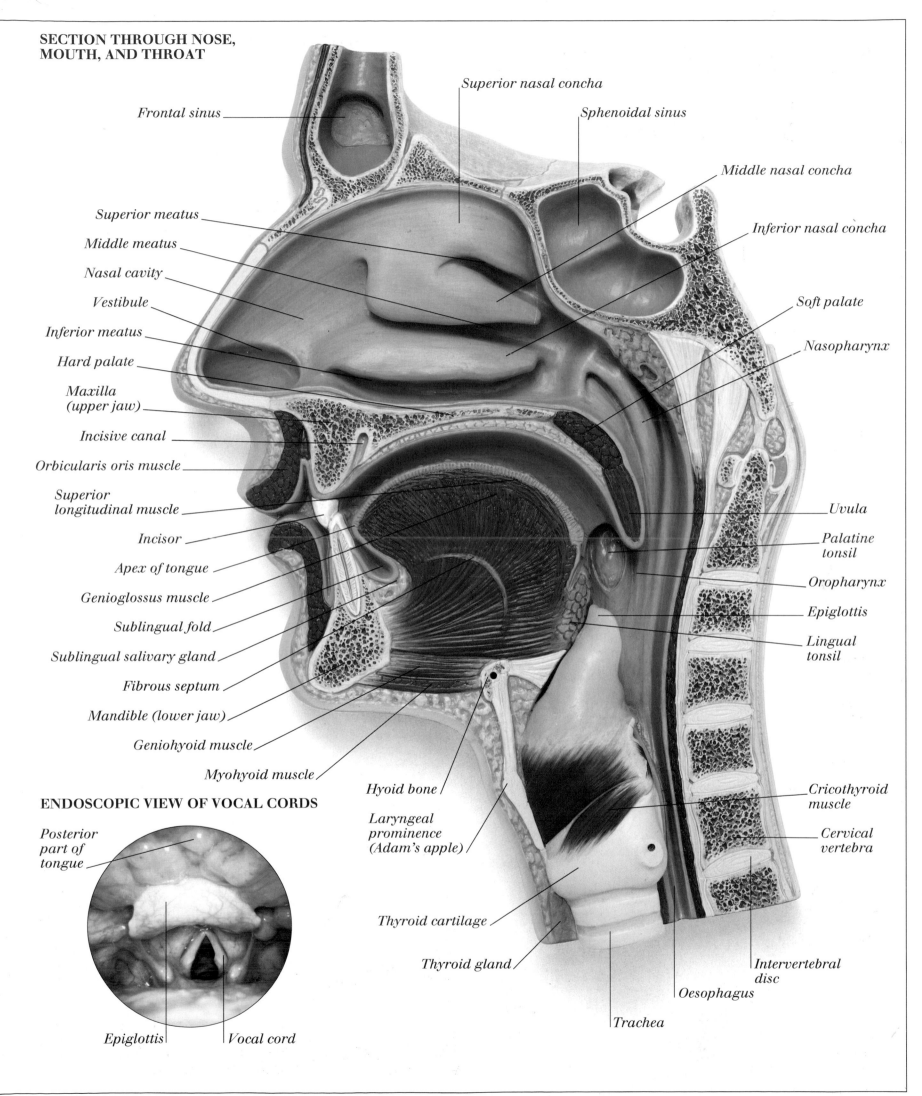

Frontal sinus

Superior nasal concha

Sphenoidal sinus

Middle nasal concha

Inferior nasal concha

Superior meatus

Middle meatus

Nasal cavity

Vestibule

Inferior meatus

Hard palate

Soft palate

Nasopharynx

Maxilla (upper jaw)

Incisive canal

Orbicularis oris muscle

Superior longitudinal muscle

Incisor

Apex of tongue

Genioglossus muscle

Sublingual fold

Sublingual salivary gland

Fibrous septum

Mandible (lower jaw)

Geniohyoid muscle

Myohyoid muscle

Uvula

Palatine tonsil

Oropharynx

Epiglottis

Lingual tonsil

ENDOSCOPIC VIEW OF VOCAL CORDS

Posterior part of tongue

Epiglottis

Vocal cord

Hyoid bone

Laryngeal prominence (Adam's apple)

Thyroid cartilage

Thyroid gland

Cricothyroid muscle

Cervical vertebra

Intervertebral disc

Oesophagus

Trachea

Teeth

THE 20 PRIMARY TEETH (also called deciduous or milk teeth) usually begin to erupt when a baby is about six months old. They start to be replaced by the permanent teeth when the child is about six years old. By the age of 20, most adults have a full set of 32 teeth although the third molars (commonly called wisdom teeth) may never erupt. While teeth help people to speak clearly and give shape to the face, their main function is the chewing of food. Incisors and canines shear and tear the food into pieces; premolars and molars crush and grind it further. Although tooth enamel is the hardest substance in the body, it tends to be eroded and destroyed by acid produced in the mouth during the breakdown of food.

DEVELOPMENT OF TEETH IN A FETUS

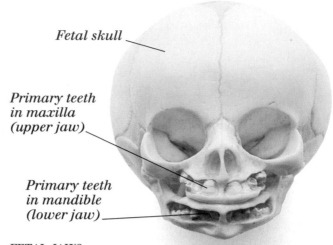

Fetal skull

Primary teeth in maxilla (upper jaw)

Primary teeth in mandible (lower jaw)

FETAL JAWS
By the sixth week of embryonic development areas of thickening occur in each jaw; these areas give rise to tooth buds. By the time the fetus is six months old, enamel has formed on the tooth buds.

DEVELOPMENT OF JAW AND TEETH

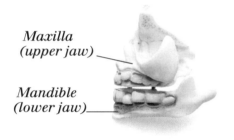
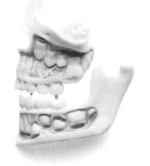
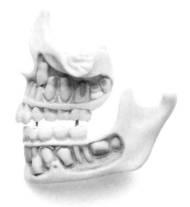
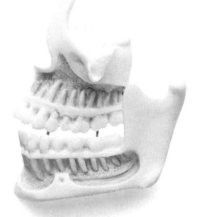

Maxilla (upper jaw)

Mandible (lower jaw)

A NEWBORN BABY'S JAWS
The primary teeth can be seen developing in the jaw bones; they begin to erupt around the age of six months.

A FIVE-YEAR-OLD CHILD'S TEETH
There is a full set of 20 erupted primary teeth; the permanent teeth can be seen developing in the upper and lower jaws.

A NINE-YEAR-OLD CHILD'S TEETH
Most of the teeth are primary teeth but the permanent incisors and first molars have now emerged.

AN ADULT'S TEETH
By the age of 20, the full set of 32 permanent teeth (including the wisdom teeth) should be in position.

THE PERMANENT TEETH

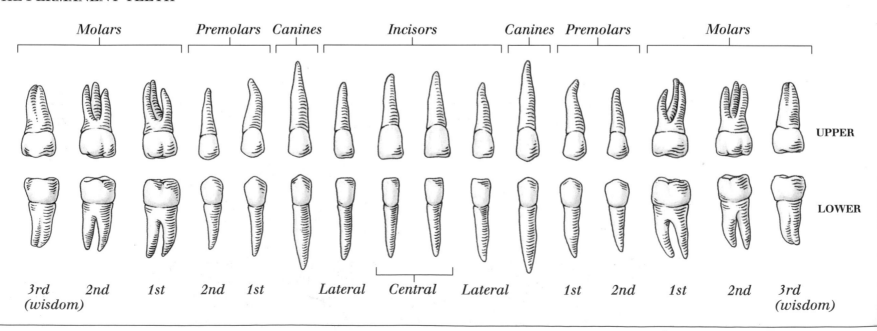

Molars | Premolars | Canines | Incisors | Canines | Premolars | Molars

UPPER

LOWER

3rd (wisdom) | 2nd | 1st | 2nd | 1st | Lateral | Central | Lateral | 1st | 2nd | 1st | 2nd | 3rd (wisdom)

STRUCTURE OF A TOOTH

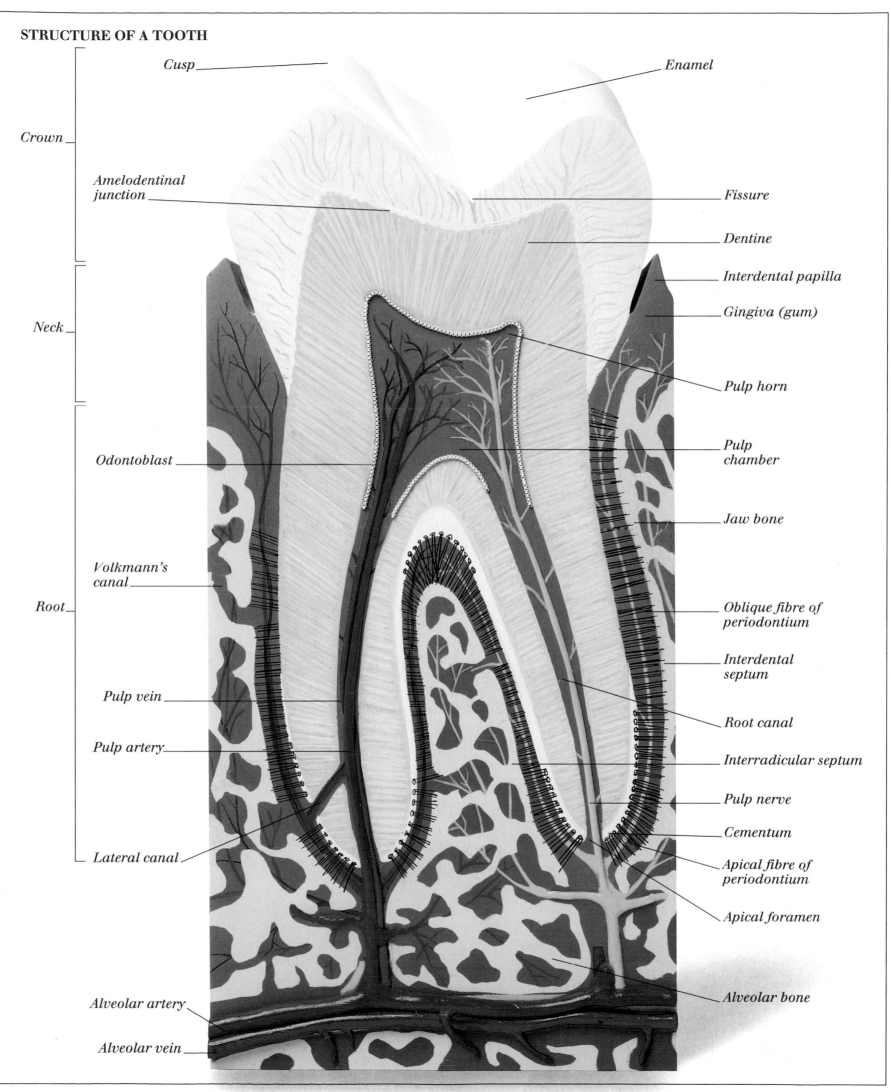

Cusp

Enamel

Crown

Amelodentinal junction

Fissure

Dentine

Interdental papilla

Neck

Gingiva (gum)

Pulp horn

Odontoblast

Pulp chamber

Jaw bone

Volkmann's canal

Oblique fibre of periodontium

Root

Interdental septum

Pulp vein

Root canal

Interradicular septum

Pulp artery

Pulp nerve

Cementum

Lateral canal

Apical fibre of periodontium

Apical foramen

Alveolar bone

Alveolar artery

Alveolar vein

Digestive system 1

THE DIGESTIVE SYSTEM BREAKS DOWN FOOD into particles so tiny that blood can take nourishment to all parts of the body. The system's main part is a 9 m (30 ft) tube from mouth to rectum; muscles in this alimentary canal force food along. Chewed food first travels through the oesophagus to the stomach, which churns and liquidizes food before it passes through the duodenum, jejunum, and ileum – the three parts of the long, convoluted small intestine. Here, digestive juices from the gallbladder and pancreas break down food particles; many filter out into the blood through tiny fingerlike villi that line the small intestine's inner wall. Undigested food in the colon forms faeces that leave the body through the anus.

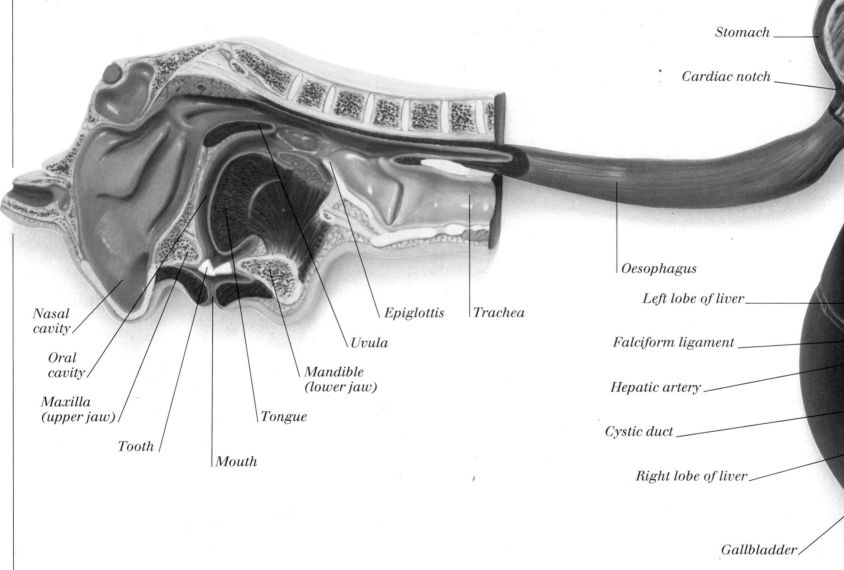

Stomach

Cardiac notch

Oesophagus

Left lobe of liver

Falciform ligament

Hepatic artery

Cystic duct

Right lobe of liver

Gallbladder

Nasal cavity

Oral cavity

Maxilla (upper jaw)

Tooth

Mouth

Tongue

Mandible (lower jaw)

Uvula

Epiglottis

Trachea

ENDOSCOPIC VIEWS INSIDE ALIMENTARY CANAL

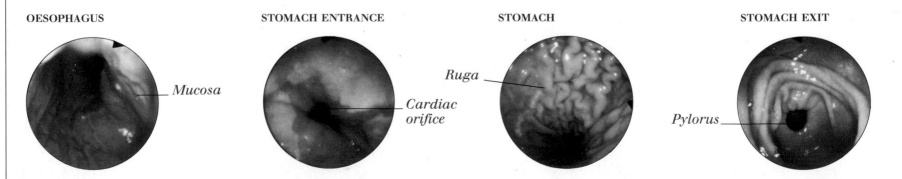

OESOPHAGUS

Mucosa

STOMACH ENTRANCE

Cardiac orifice

STOMACH

Ruga

STOMACH EXIT

Pylorus

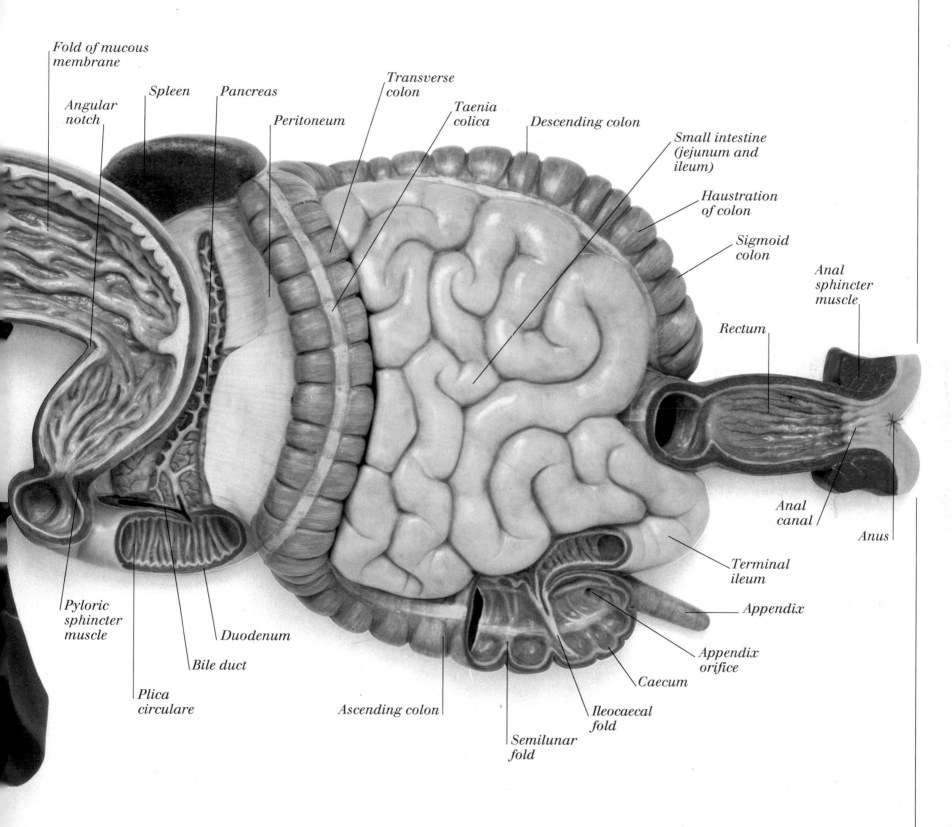

Fold of mucous membrane

Angular notch

Spleen

Pancreas

Peritoneum

Transverse colon

Taenia colica

Descending colon

Small intestine (jejunum and ileum)

Haustration of colon

Sigmoid colon

Anal sphincter muscle

Rectum

Anal canal

Anus

Terminal ileum

Appendix

Appendix orifice

Caecum

Ileocaecal fold

Semilunar fold

Ascending colon

Plica circulare

Bile duct

Duodenum

Pyloric sphincter muscle

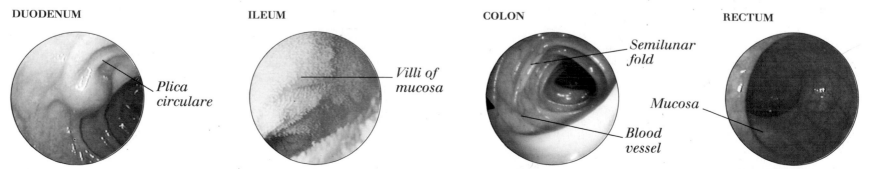

DUODENUM

Plica circulare

ILEUM

Villi of mucosa

COLON

Semilunar fold

Blood vessel

RECTUM

Mucosa

Digestive system 2

STRUCTURE OF ALIMENTARY CANAL
SECTION OF OESOPHAGEAL WALL

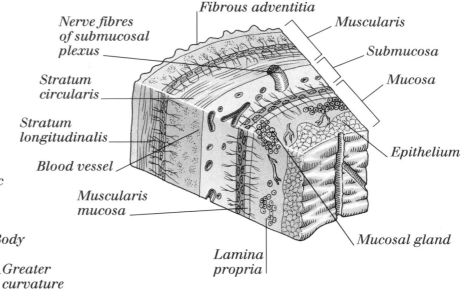

Nerve fibres of submucosal plexus

Fibrous adventitia

Muscularis

Submucosa

Mucosa

Stratum circularis

Stratum longitudinalis

Blood vessel

Epithelium

Muscularis mucosa

Mucosal gland

Lamina propria

EXTERNAL ANATOMY OF STOMACH

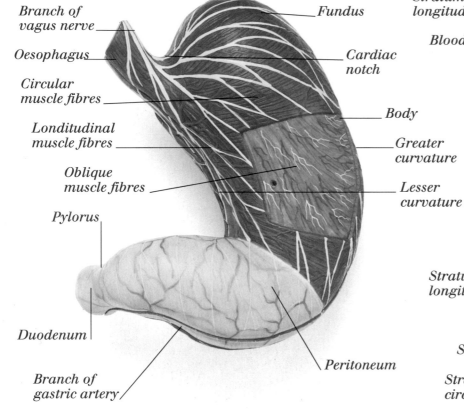

Branch of vagus nerve

Fundus

Oesophagus

Cardiac notch

Circular muscle fibres

Londitudinal muscle fibres

Body

Oblique muscle fibres

Greater curvature

Pylorus

Lesser curvature

Duodenum

Branch of gastric artery

Peritoneum

SECTION OF STOMACH WALL

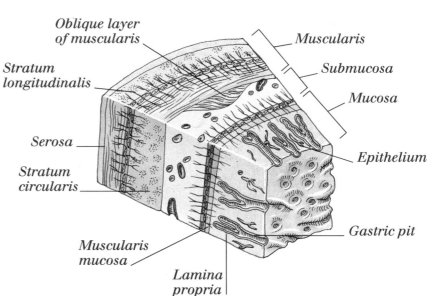

Oblique layer of muscularis

Muscularis

Submucosa

Stratum longitudinalis

Mucosa

Serosa

Stratum circularis

Epithelium

Muscularis mucosa

Gastric pit

Lamina propria

SECTION THROUGH LIVER

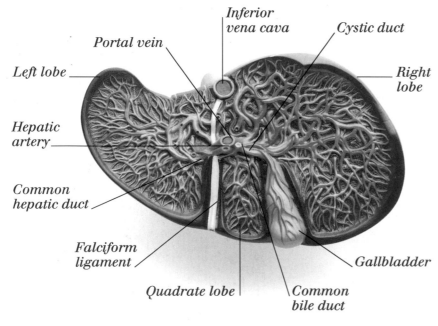

Inferior vena cava

Portal vein

Cystic duct

Left lobe

Right lobe

Hepatic artery

Common hepatic duct

Falciform ligament

Gallbladder

Quadrate lobe

Common bile duct

SECTION OF DUODENAL WALL

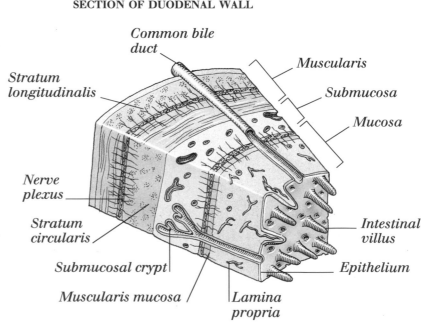

Common bile duct

Muscularis

Stratum longitudinalis

Submucosa

Mucosa

Nerve plexus

Stratum circularis

Intestinal villus

Submucosal crypt

Epithelium

Muscularis mucosa

Lamina propria

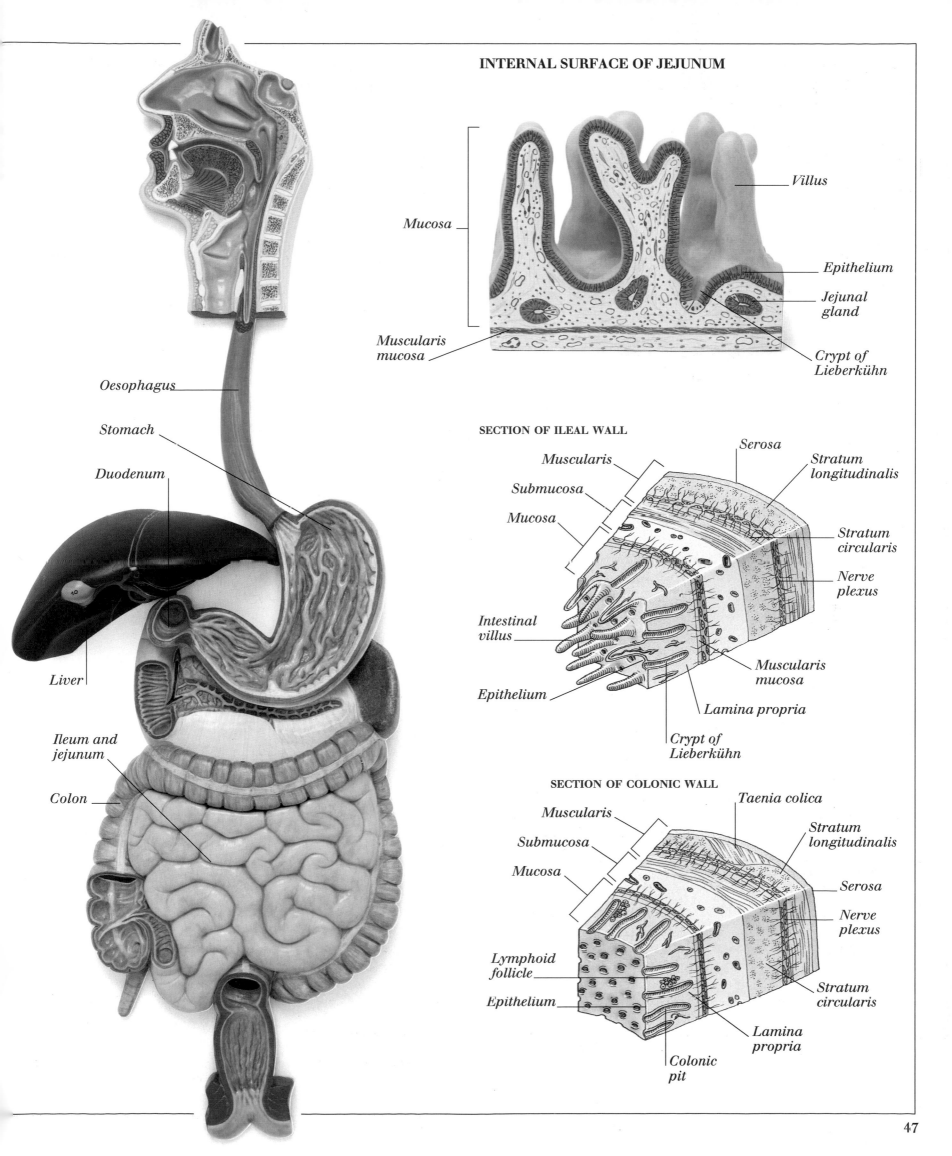

INTERNAL SURFACE OF JEJUNUM

Villus

Mucosa

Epithelium

Jejunal gland

Muscularis mucosa

Crypt of Lieberkühn

Oesophagus

Stomach

Duodenum

Liver

Ileum and jejunum

Colon

SECTION OF ILEAL WALL

Muscularis

Submucosa

Mucosa

Serosa

Stratum longitudinalis

Stratum circularis

Nerve plexus

Intestinal villus

Epithelium

Muscularis mucosa

Lamina propria

Crypt of Lieberkühn

SECTION OF COLONIC WALL

Muscularis

Submucosa

Mucosa

Taenia colica

Stratum longitudinalis

Serosa

Nerve plexus

Lymphoid follicle

Epithelium

Stratum circularis

Lamina propria

Colonic pit

Heart

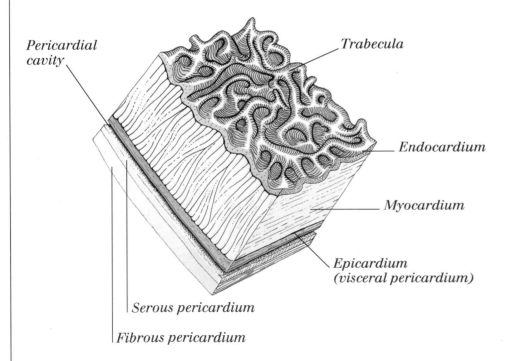

THE HEART IS A HOLLOW MUSCLE in the middle of the chest that pumps blood around the body, supplying cells with oxygen and nutrients. A muscular wall, called the septum, divides the heart lengthways into left and right sides. A valve divides each side into two chambers: an upper atrium and a lower ventricle. When the heart muscle contracts, it squeezes blood through the atria and then through the ventricles. Oxygenated blood from the lungs flows from the pulmonary veins into the left atrium, through the left ventricle, and then out via the aorta to all parts of the body. Deoxygenated blood returning from the body flows from the vena cava into the right atrium, through the right ventricle, and then out via the pulmonary artery to the lungs for reoxygenation. At rest the heart beats between 60 and 80 times a minute; during exercise or at times of stress or excitement the rate may increase to 200 beats a minute.

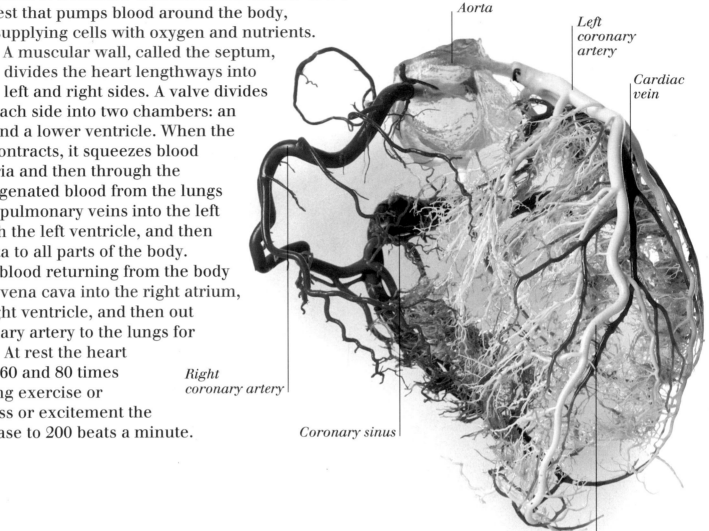

Aorta

Left coronary artery

Cardiac vein

Right coronary artery

Coronary sinus

Main branch of left coronary artery

SECTION THROUGH HEART WALL

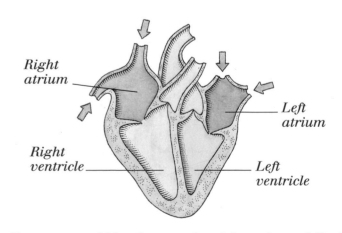

Pericardial cavity

Trabecula

Endocardium

Myocardium

Epicardium (visceral pericardium)

Serous pericardium

Fibrous pericardium

HEARTBEAT SEQUENCE

ATRIAL DIASTOLE

Right atrium

Left atrium

Right ventricle

Left ventricle

Deoxygenated blood enters the right atrium while the left atrium receives oxygenated blood.

48

STRUCTURE OF HEART

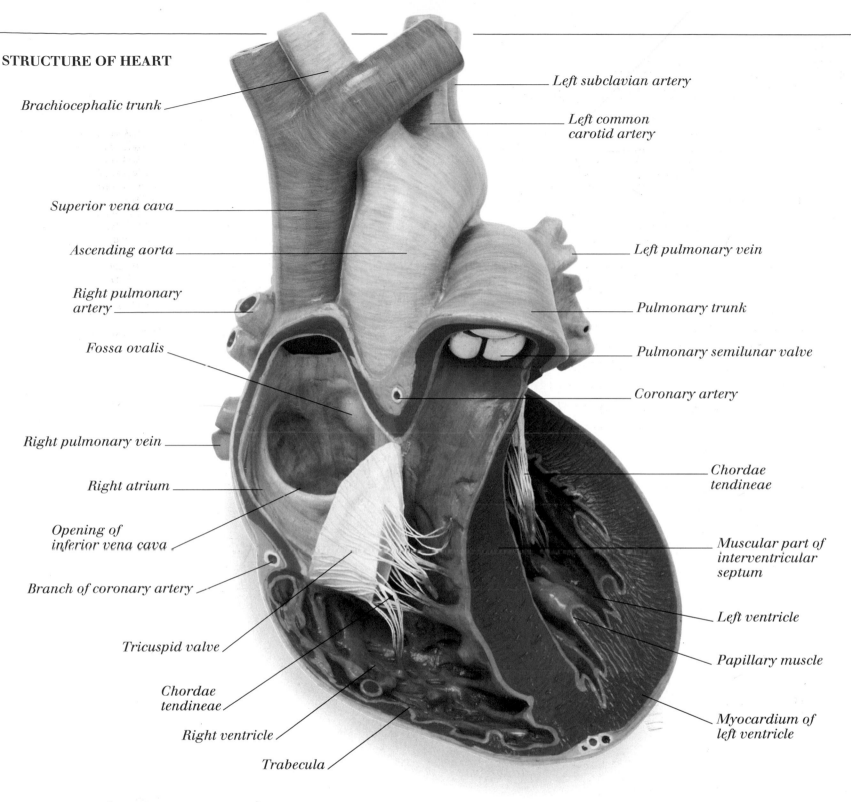

Brachiocephalic trunk

Left subclavian artery

Left common carotid artery

Superior vena cava

Ascending aorta

Left pulmonary vein

Right pulmonary artery

Pulmonary trunk

Fossa ovalis

Pulmonary semilunar valve

Coronary artery

Right pulmonary vein

Right atrium

Chordae tendineae

Opening of inferior vena cava

Muscular part of interventricular septum

Branch of coronary artery

Left ventricle

Tricuspid valve

Papillary muscle

Chordae tendineae

Right ventricle

Myocardium of left ventricle

Trabecula

ATRIAL SYSTOLE (VENTRICULAR DIASTOLE)

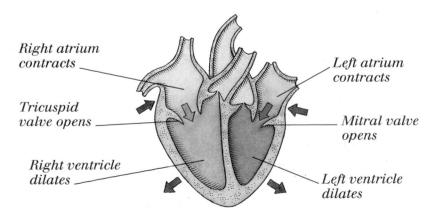

Right atrium contracts

Left atrium contracts

Tricuspid valve opens

Mitral valve opens

Right ventricle dilates

Left ventricle dilates

Left and right atria contract, forcing blood into the relaxed ventricles.

VENTRICULAR SYSTOLE

Pulmonary artery

Aorta

Pulmonary valve opens

Aortic valve opens

Tricuspid valve closes

Mitral valve closes

Right ventricle contracts

Left ventricle contracts

Ventricles contract and force blood to the lungs for oxygenation and via the aorta to the rest of the body.

Circulatory system

THE CIRCULATORY SYSTEM consists of the heart and blood vessels, which together maintain a continuous flow of blood around the body. The heart pumps oxygen-rich blood from the lungs to all parts of the body through a network of tubes called arteries, and smaller branches called arterioles. Blood returns to the heart via small vessels called venules, which lead in turn into larger tubes called veins. Arterioles and venules are linked by a network of tiny vessels called capillaries, where the exchange of oxygen and carbon dioxide between blood and body cells takes place. Blood has four main components: red blood cells, white blood cells, platelets, and liquid plasma.

ARTERIAL SYSTEM OF BRAIN

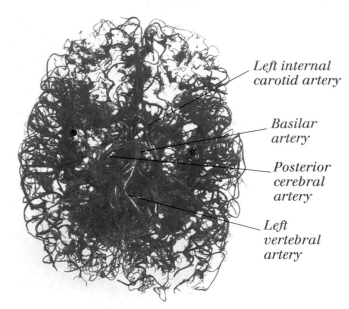

Left internal carotid artery

Basilar artery

Posterior cerebral artery

Left vertebral artery

CIRCULATORY SYSTEM OF HEART AND LUNGS

Superior vena cava

Aorta

Right ventricle

Left ventricle

CIRCULATORY SYSTEM OF LIVER

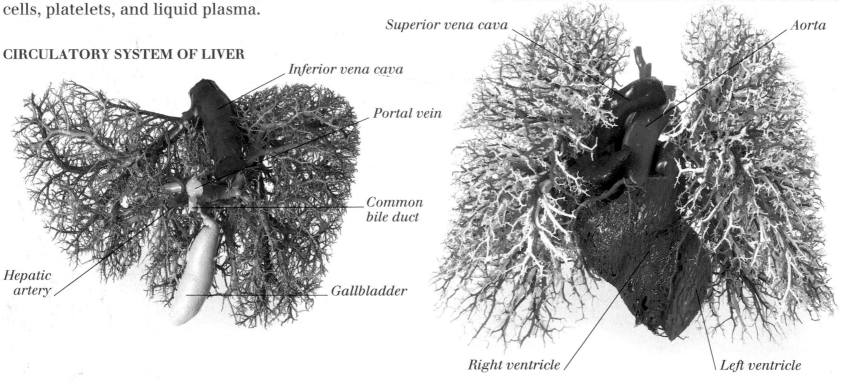

Inferior vena cava

Portal vein

Common bile duct

Hepatic artery

Gallbladder

SECTION OF MAIN ARTERY

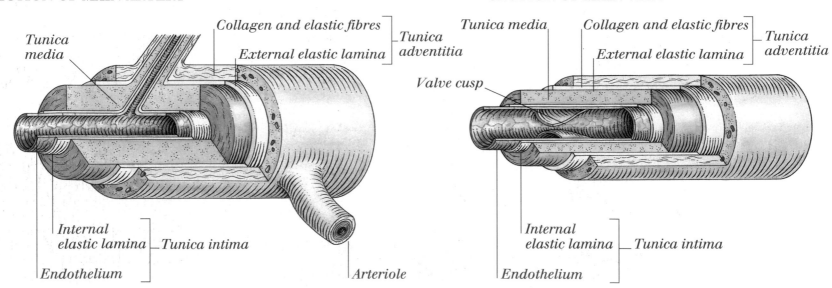

Tunica media

Collagen and elastic fibres

External elastic lamina

Tunica adventitia

Internal elastic lamina

Tunica intima

Endothelium

Arteriole

SECTION OF MAIN VEIN

Tunica media

Collagen and elastic fibres

External elastic lamina

Tunica adventitia

Valve cusp

Internal elastic lamina

Tunica intima

Endothelium

PRINCIPAL ARTERIES AND VEINS OF CIRCULATORY SYSTEM

Common carotid artery

Subclavian artery

Arch of aorta

Axillary artery

Pulmonary artery

Coronary artery

Brachial artery

Gastric artery

Hepatic artery

Splenic artery

Superior mesenteric artery

Radial artery

Ulnar artery

Palmar arch

Digital artery

Common iliac artery

External iliac artery

Internal iliac artery

Femoral artery

Popliteal artery

Peroneal artery

Anterior tibial artery

Posterior tibial artery

Lateral plantar artery

Dorsal metatarsal artery

Internal jugular vein

Brachiocephalic vein

Subclavian vein

Axillary vein

Cephalic vein

Superior vena cava

Pulmonary vein

Basilic vein

Hepatic portal vein

Median cubital vein

Inferior vena cava

Anterior median vein

Gastroepiploic vein

Palmar vein

Digital vein

Inferior mesenteric vein

Superior mesenteric vein

Common iliac vein

External iliac vein

Internal iliac vein

Femoral vein

Great saphenous vein

Short saphenous vein

Dorsal venous arch

Digital vein

TYPES OF BLOOD CELLS

RED BLOOD CELLS
These cells are biconcave in shape to maximize their oxygen-carrying capacity.

WHITE BLOOD CELLS
Lymphocytes are the smallest white blood cells; they form antibodies against disease.

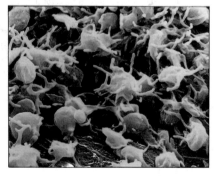

PLATELETS
Tiny cells that are activated whenever blood clotting or repair to vessels is necessary.

BLOOD CLOTTING

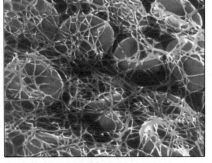

Filaments of fibrin enmesh red blood cells as part of the process of blood clotting.

Respiratory system

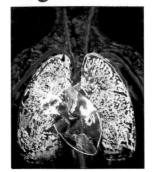

THE RESPIRATORY SYSTEM supplies the oxygen needed by body cells and carries off their carbon dioxide waste. Inhaled air passes via the trachea (windpipe) through two narrower tubes, the bronchi, to the lungs. Each lung comprises many fine, branching tubes called bronchioles that end in tiny clustered chambers called alveoli. Gases cross the thin alveolar walls to and from a network of tiny blood vessels. Intercostal (rib) muscles and the muscular diaphragm below the lungs operate the lungs like bellows, drawing air in and forcing it out at regular intervals.

BRONCHIOLE AND ALVEOLI

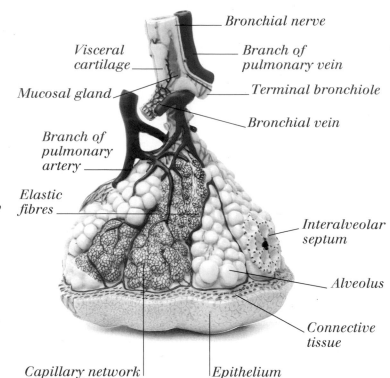

- Bronchial nerve
- Visceral cartilage
- Branch of pulmonary vein
- Terminal bronchiole
- Mucosal gland
- Bronchial vein
- Branch of pulmonary artery
- Elastic fibres
- Interalveolar septum
- Alveolus
- Connective tissue
- Capillary network
- Epithelium

SEGMENTS OF BRONCHIAL TREE

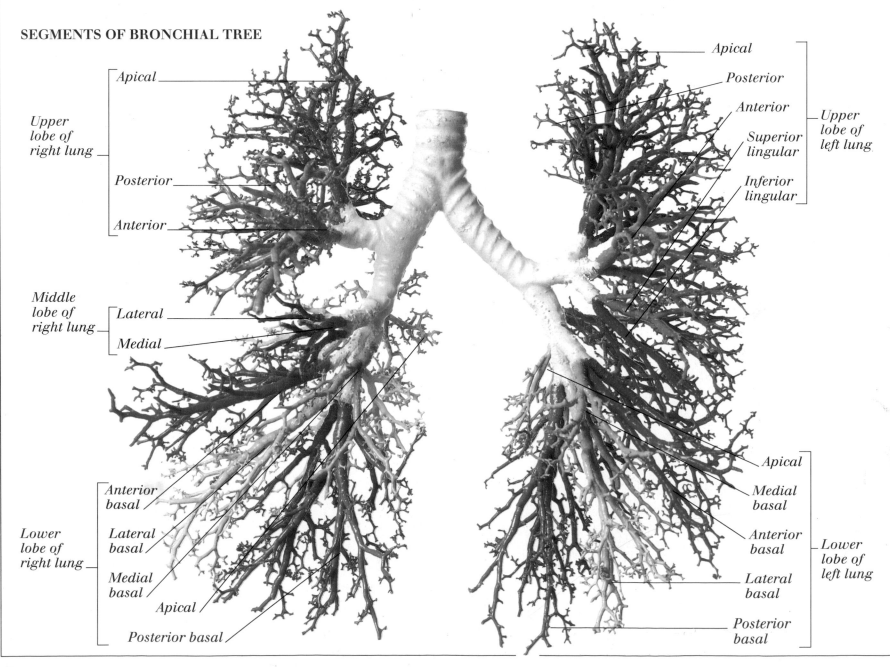

- Apical
- Upper lobe of right lung
- Posterior
- Anterior
- Middle lobe of right lung
- Lateral
- Medial
- Anterior basal
- Lateral basal
- Lower lobe of right lung
- Medial basal
- Apical
- Posterior basal

- Apical
- Posterior
- Anterior
- Superior lingular
- Upper lobe of left lung
- Inferior lingular
- Apical
- Medial basal
- Anterior basal
- Lower lobe of left lung
- Lateral basal
- Posterior basal

STRUCTURES OF THORACIC CAVITY

Epiglottis

Hyoid bone

Thyroid cartilage

Thyroid gland

Apex of lung

Superior vena cava

Upper lobe of right lung

Horizontal fissure

Oblique fissure

Cricoid cartilage

Trachea

Aorta

Upper lobe of left lung

Pulmonary trunk

Left pulmonary artery

Heart

Lower lobe of left lung

Secondary bronchus

Tertiary bronchus

Lower lobe of right lung

Middle lobe of right lung

Right crus of diaphragm

Abdominal aorta

Left crus of diaphragm

Oesophagus

Muscular wall of diaphragm

GASEOUS EXCHANGE IN ALVEOLUS

Oxygen diffuses into blood

Oxygenated blood

Alveolus

Deoxygenated blood rich in carbon dioxide

Carbon dioxide diffuses from blood into alveolus

MECHANISM OF RESPIRATION
INSPIRATION

Lung expands

Air drawn into lungs

Diaphragm contracts and flattens

Intercostal muscles contract

EXPIRATION

Lung contracts

Air forced out of lungs

Diaphragm relaxes and moves up

Intercostal muscles relax

Urinary system

THE URINARY SYSTEM FILTERS WASTE PRODUCTS from the blood and removes them from the body via a system of tubes. Blood is filtered in the two kidneys, which are fist-sized, bean-shaped organs. The renal arteries carry blood to the kidneys; the renal veins remove blood after filtering. Each kidney contains about one million tiny units called nephrons. Each nephron is made up of a tubule and a filtering unit called a glomerulus, which consists of a collection of tiny blood vessels surrounded by the hollow Bowman's capsule. The filtering process produces a watery fluid that leaves the kidney as urine. The urine is carried via two tubes called ureters to the bladder, where it is stored until its release from the body through another tube called the urethra.

ARTERIAL SYSTEM OF KIDNEYS

Aorta

Coeliac trunk

Superior mesenteric artery

Right renal artery

Left renal artery

Right ureter

Left ureter

SECTION THROUGH LEFT KIDNEY

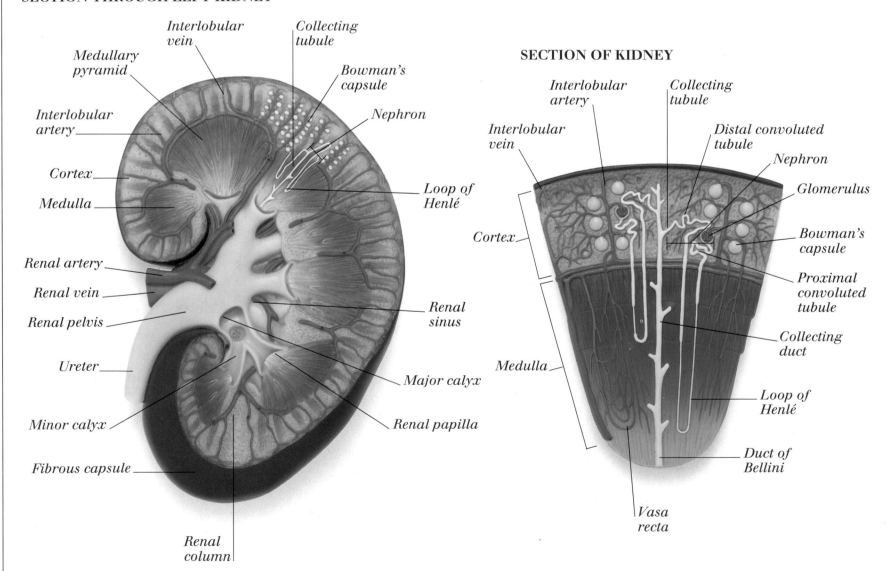

Interlobular vein

Collecting tubule

Medullary pyramid

Bowman's capsule

Interlobular artery

Nephron

Cortex

Medulla

Loop of Henlé

Renal artery

Renal vein

Renal pelvis

Renal sinus

Ureter

Major calyx

Minor calyx

Renal papilla

Fibrous capsule

Renal column

SECTION OF KIDNEY

Interlobular artery

Collecting tubule

Interlobular vein

Distal convoluted tubule

Nephron

Cortex

Glomerulus

Bowman's capsule

Proximal convoluted tubule

Medulla

Collecting duct

Loop of Henlé

Duct of Bellini

Vasa recta

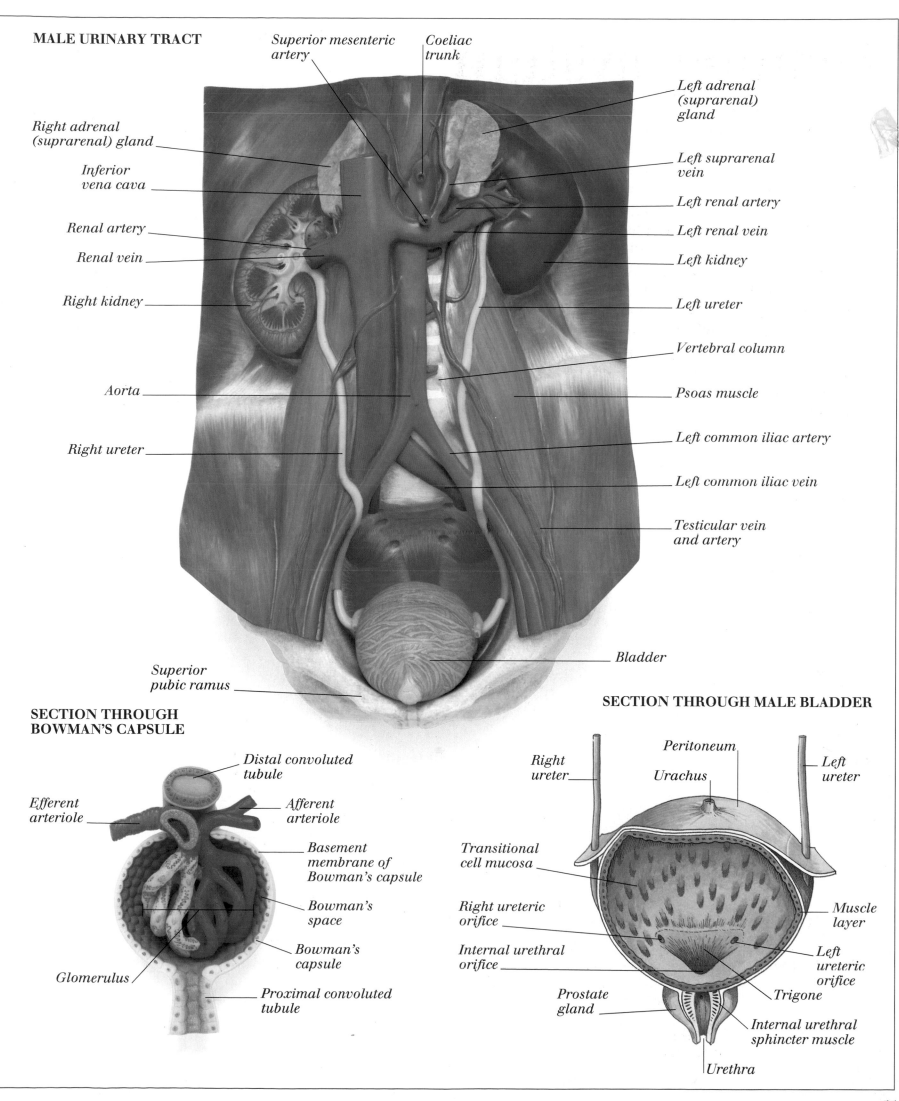

MALE URINARY TRACT

Superior mesenteric artery

Coeliac trunk

Left adrenal (suprarenal) gland

Right adrenal (suprarenal) gland

Inferior vena cava

Renal artery

Renal vein

Right kidney

Aorta

Right ureter

Superior pubic ramus

Left suprarenal vein

Left renal artery

Left renal vein

Left kidney

Left ureter

Vertebral column

Psoas muscle

Left common iliac artery

Left common iliac vein

Testicular vein and artery

Bladder

SECTION THROUGH BOWMAN'S CAPSULE

Distal convoluted tubule

Efferent arteriole

Afferent arteriole

Basement membrane of Bowman's capsule

Bowman's space

Bowman's capsule

Glomerulus

Proximal convoluted tubule

SECTION THROUGH MALE BLADDER

Peritoneum

Right ureter

Urachus

Left ureter

Transitional cell mucosa

Right ureteric orifice

Internal urethral orifice

Muscle layer

Left ureteric orifice

Prostate gland

Trigone

Internal urethral sphincter muscle

Urethra

Reproductive system

SEX ORGANS LOCATED IN THE PELVIS create new human lives. Each month a ripe egg is released from one of the female's ovaries into a fallopian tube leading to the uterus (womb), a muscular pear-sized organ. A male produces minute tadpole-like sperm in two oval glands called testes. When the male is ready to release sperm into the female's vagina, many millions pass into his urethra and leave his body through the fleshy penis. The sperm travel up through the vagina into the uterus and one sperm may enter and fertilize an egg. The fertilized egg becomes embedded in the uterus wall and starts to grow into a new human being.

SECTION THROUGH OVARY

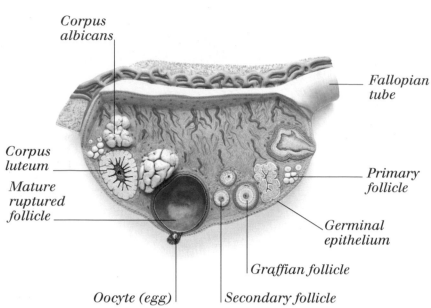

Corpus albicans

Fallopian tube

Corpus luteum

Mature ruptured follicle

Primary follicle

Germinal epithelium

Graffian follicle

Oocyte (egg)

Secondary follicle

SECTION THROUGH FEMALE PELVIC REGION

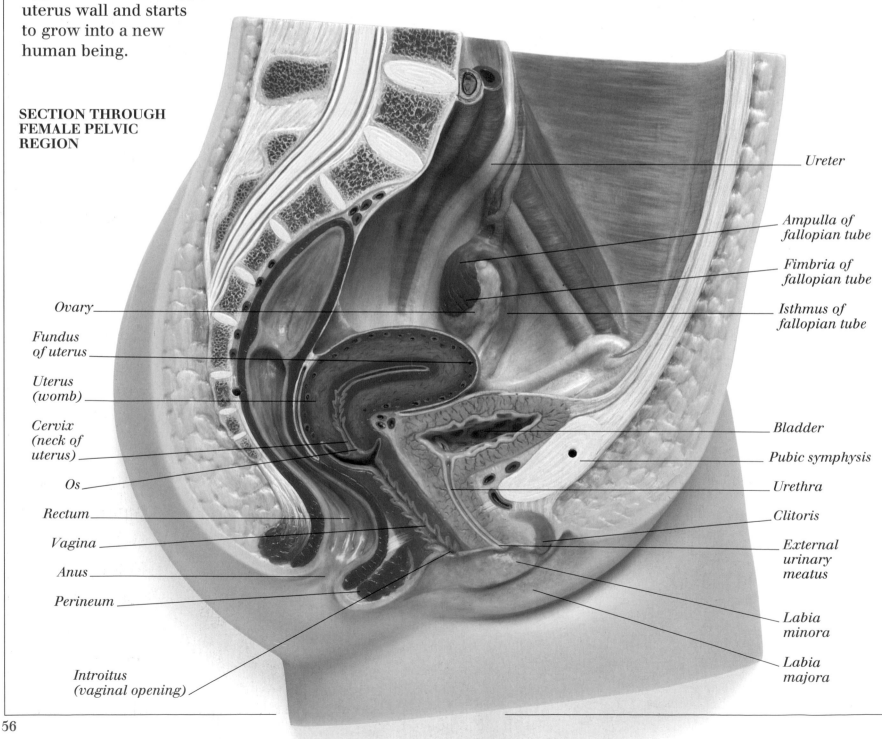

Ureter

Ampulla of fallopian tube

Fimbria of fallopian tube

Isthmus of fallopian tube

Ovary

Fundus of uterus

Uterus (womb)

Cervix (neck of uterus)

Os

Rectum

Vagina

Anus

Perineum

Introitus (vaginal opening)

Bladder

Pubic symphysis

Urethra

Clitoris

External urinary meatus

Labia minora

Labia majora

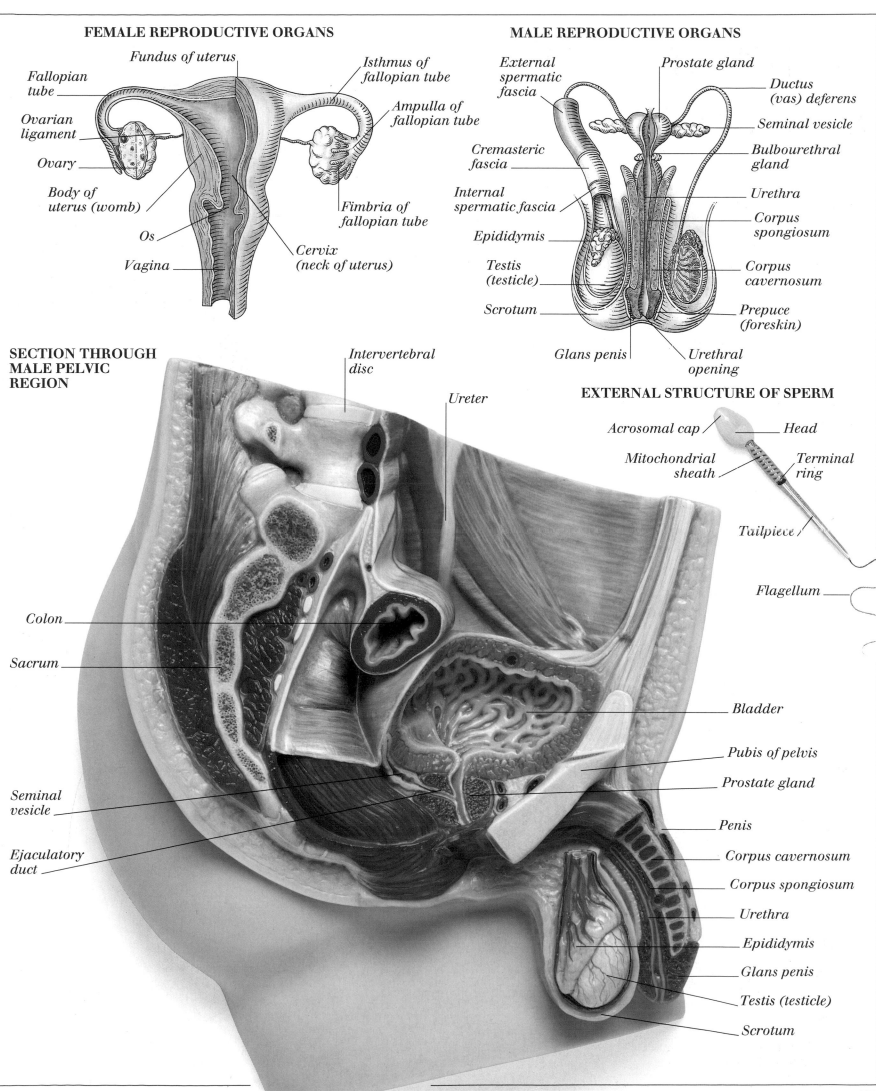

FEMALE REPRODUCTIVE ORGANS

Fundus of uterus

Fallopian tube

Isthmus of fallopian tube

Ovarian ligament

Ampulla of fallopian tube

Ovary

Body of uterus (womb)

Os

Fimbria of fallopian tube

Cervix (neck of uterus)

Vagina

MALE REPRODUCTIVE ORGANS

External spermatic fascia

Prostate gland

Ductus (vas) deferens

Seminal vesicle

Cremasteric fascia

Bulbourethral gland

Internal spermatic fascia

Urethra

Epididymis

Corpus spongiosum

Testis (testicle)

Corpus cavernosum

Scrotum

Prepuce (foreskin)

Glans penis

Urethral opening

SECTION THROUGH MALE PELVIC REGION

Intervertebral disc

Ureter

Colon

Sacrum

Seminal vesicle

Ejaculatory duct

Bladder

Pubis of pelvis

Prostate gland

Penis

Corpus cavernosum

Corpus spongiosum

Urethra

Epididymis

Glans penis

Testis (testicle)

Scrotum

EXTERNAL STRUCTURE OF SPERM

Acrosomal cap

Head

Mitochondrial sheath

Terminal ring

Tailpiece

Flagellum

Development of a baby

A FERTILIZED EGG IS NOURISHED AND PROTECTED as it develops into an embryo and then a fetus during the 40 weeks of pregnancy. The placenta, a mass of blood vessels implanted in the uterus lining, delivers nourishment and oxygen, and removes waste through the umbilical cord. Meanwhile, the fetus lies snugly in its amniotic sac, a bag of fluid that protects it against any sudden jolts. In the last weeks of the pregnancy, the rapidly growing fetus turns head-down: a baby ready to be born.

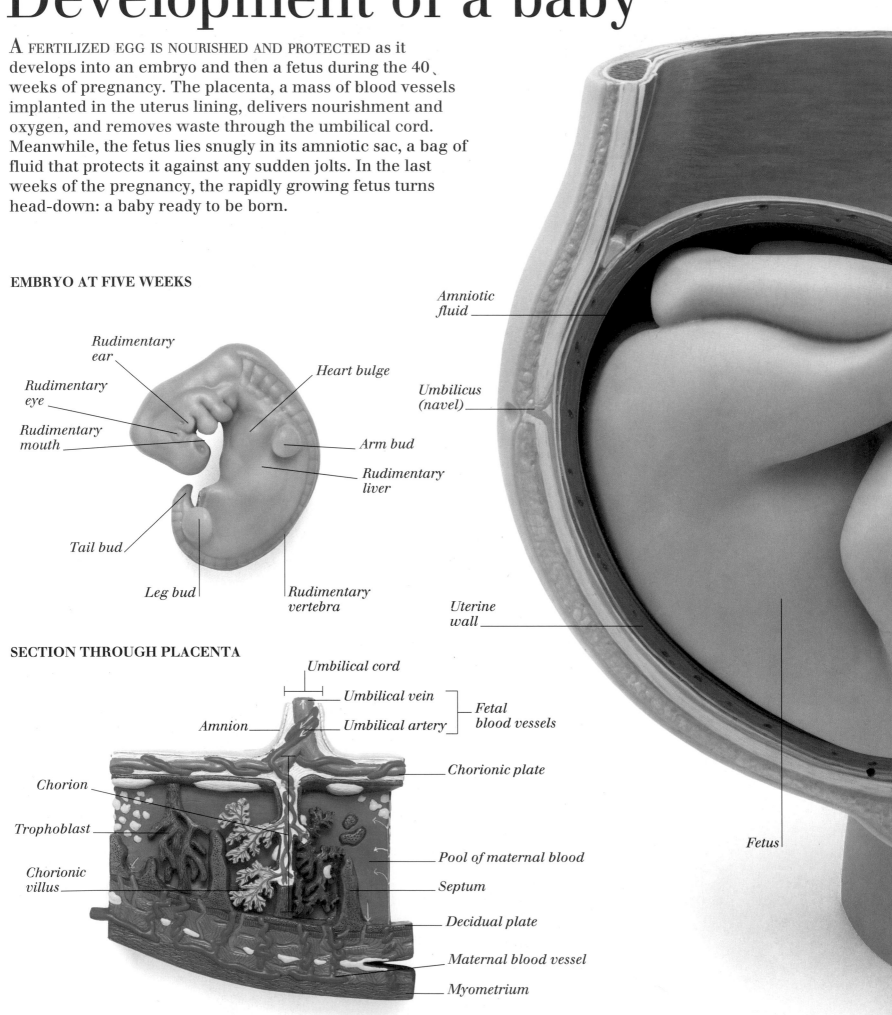

EMBRYO AT FIVE WEEKS

Rudimentary ear

Rudimentary eye

Rudimentary mouth

Heart bulge

Arm bud

Rudimentary liver

Tail bud

Leg bud

Rudimentary vertebra

Amniotic fluid

Umbilicus (navel)

Uterine wall

Fetus

SECTION THROUGH PLACENTA

Umbilical cord

Umbilical vein

Umbilical artery

Fetal blood vessels

Amnion

Chorionic plate

Chorion

Trophoblast

Chorionic villus

Pool of maternal blood

Septum

Decidual plate

Maternal blood vessel

Myometrium

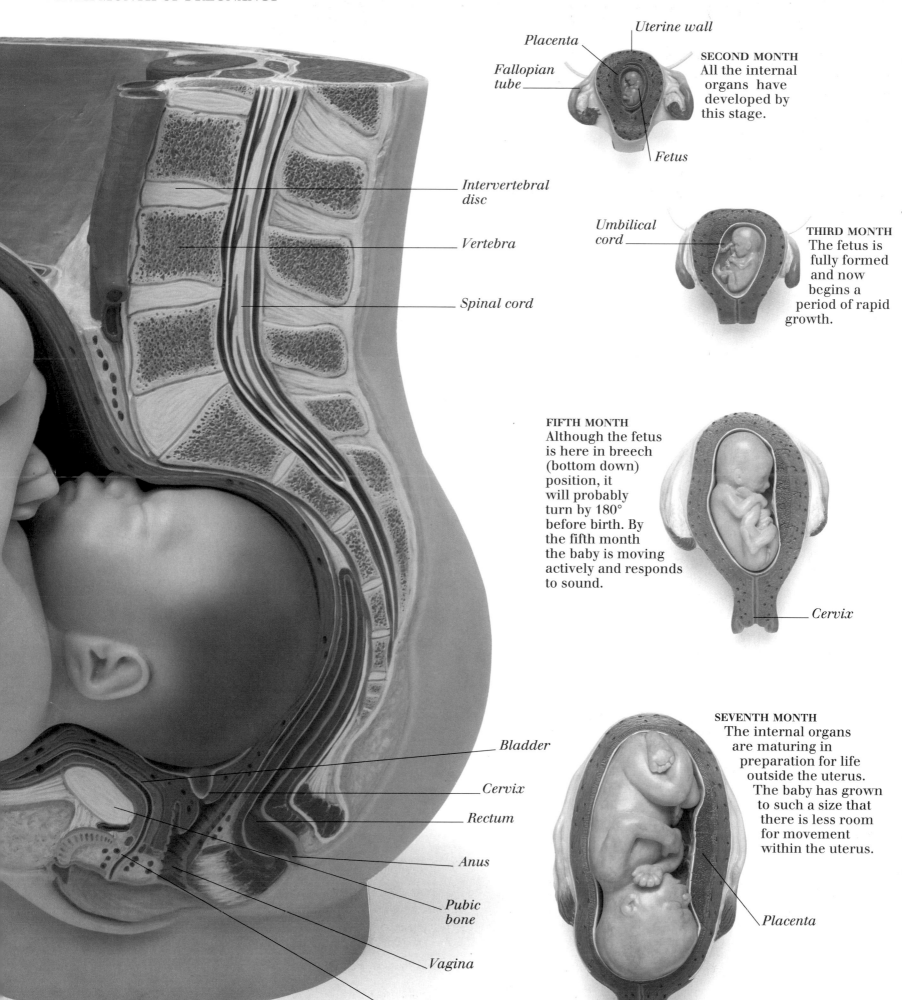

SECTION THROUGH PELVIS IN NINTH MONTH OF PREGNANCY

THE DEVELOPING FETUS

Intervertebral disc

Vertebra

Spinal cord

Bladder

Cervix

Rectum

Anus

Pubic bone

Vagina

Urethra

Placenta

Uterine wall

Fallopian tube

Fetus

SECOND MONTH
All the internal organs have developed by this stage.

Umbilical cord

THIRD MONTH
The fetus is fully formed and now begins a period of rapid growth.

FIFTH MONTH
Although the fetus is here in breech (bottom down) position, it will probably turn by 180° before birth. By the fifth month the baby is moving actively and responds to sound.

Cervix

SEVENTH MONTH
The internal organs are maturing in preparation for life outside the uterus. The baby has grown to such a size that there is less room for movement within the uterus.

Placenta

Index

Acknowledgments

Dorling Kindersley would like to thank :
Derek Edwards and Dr Martin Collins, British School of Osteopathy for skeletal material and advice; Dr M.C.E. Hutchinson, Department of Anatomy, United Medical and Dental Schools of Guy's and St Thomas' Hospitals for resin casts, additional skeletal material, and advice; models Barry O'Rorke (Bodyline Agency) and Pauline Swaine (MOT Model Agency).

Additional editorial assistance:
Susan Bosanko, Candace Burch, Deirdre Clark, Paul Docherty, Edwina Johnson, David Lambert, Gail Lawther, Dr Robert Youngson

Additional models
Bodyline, Donkin Models, Gordon Models, Morrison Frederick

Additional photography:
Dave Rudkin

Illustrators:
Simone End, Roy Flooks, David Gardner, Mick Gillah, Dave Hopkins, Linden Artists, John Woodcock

Index:
Dr Robert Youngson

Picture credits:
a=above, b=below, c=centre, J=jacket, l=left, m=middle, r=right, t=top
Biophoto Associates: pages 13ca, cra, 24cbc, cbm, 26tr
KeyMed Ltd: 44bl, 45bl, bcl
Dr D.N. Landon (Institute of Neurology): 24bl, br
Life Science Images (Ron Boardman): 40bl, br
National Medical Slide Bank: 13cr

Science Photo Library: 10brc, 32; /Michael Abbey: 21t; /Agfa: Jct, 16tl; /Biophoto Associates: 13crb; /Dr Jeremy Burgess: 31bcl; /CNRI:10tl, cl, c, cr, bl, clb, crb, blc, br, 13cb, 31bcr, 34tl, 45bcr, 51tr, cra, 54tl; / Dr Brian Eyden: 24cbr; /Professor C. Ferlaud: 41clb; / Simon Fraser; 10 bcl; /Eric Grave: 13br; /Jan Hinsch: 21tc; /Manfred Kage: 13c, 31br, 33b; /Astrid and Hans-Freider Michler: 13tr; /NIBSC: 51br; /Omikron: 40bc; /David Scharf: 31bl; /Dr Klaus Schiller: 44bcl, bcr, br; /Secchi-Lecaque/Roussel-UCLAF/CNRI: 13tc, 51crb;/Stammers/Thompson: 26tl; /Sheila Terry: 30tl
Dr Christopher B. Williams (St Mark's Hospital): 45br
Dr Robert Youngson: 37cr
Zefa: 13bc; /H. Sochurek: Jcb, 6tl, 10cb, bcr, 48tl, 52tl

Picture research:
Sandra Schneider